downsize

down**size**

Living large in a small house

Sheri Koones

The Taunton Press

The Taunton Press
Inspiration for hands-on living®

The Taunton Press, Inc.
63 South Main Street
Newtown, CT 06470
Email: tp@taunton.com

Editor: Peter Chapman
Copy Editor: Carolyn Mandarano
Illustrations: Charles Lockhart
Jacket/Cover design: Barbara Cottingham
Interior design: Rita Sowins / Sowins Design
Layout: Lynne Phillips
Front cover photo: Lesle Lane, Studio 13 Photography
Back cover photo: Casey Dunn
Title page photo: Poppi Photography
Facing page photo: Dale Lang
Contents page photo: Acorn Art & Photography

The following names/manufacturers appearing in *Downsize* are trademarks:
Acuity Brands®, adorne®, Amana®, Andersen®, Avanti®, Baldwin®, Benjamin Moore®, Blomberg®, Boral®, Bradford White®, Broan®, Caesarstone®, Central® Restaurant Products, Columbia®, Connecticut Screen Works®, Corning® Willow®, COR-TEN®, Crossville®, Daltile®, Danby®, DecoTech®, Emerson®, Emtek®, Essence Series®, EverGuard®, FabCab®, Facebook®, Farrow & Ball®, Feeney®, First Co.®, Frigidaire®, Gatco®, Goodwill®, Gulf Coast® Supply & Manufacturing, GulkLock™, H® Window, Habitat for Humanity®, Hi-Lite Mfg. Co.®, IKEA®, Internorm®, JamesHardie®, Jeld-Wen®, JennAir®, Juno®, Kährs®, Kenmore®, Kichler®, KitchenAid®, Knauf Insulation®, Kohler®, Leviton®, Lindal®, LivingHomes®, Lopi™, Lumens®, Margin®, Milgard®, MinkaAire®, Minka Group®, Mirabellei®, Mugnaini®, Navien®, Neptronic®, Newport Brass®, Niagara Conservation®, Northwest Door®, Nulmage®, OutBack Power™, Pella®, PentalQuartz®, Plant Prefab®, PURETI™, Raaks®, RenewAire®, RESNET®, Rheem®, Rockwool®, Rohl®, Schlage®, SeaGull Lighting®, Seattle Tile Company®, Sherwin-Williams®, Silestone®, Simple Pump™, Simpson®, Solatube®, Sonia®, Star®, Stillwater Dwellings®, Sun Xtender®, Sundog Solar™, SunPak®, Sunpower®, Superior Walls®, Thermador®, Therma-Tru®, Thermomass®, Thermory®, TOTO®, Trane®, True®, TruExterior®, UltimateAir®, Urbanfloor®, Velux®, Vespa®, Viking®, WarmBoard®, WaterSense®, Weather Shield®, Whirlpool®, Wittus®, Wolf®, ZIPsystem®

Library of Congress Cataloging-in-Publication Data

Names: Koones, Sheri, 1949- author.
Title: Downsize : living large in a small house / Sheri Koones.
Description: Newtown, CT : The Taunton Press, Inc., [2019]
Identifiers: LCCN 2019014742 | ISBN 9781641550338 (print) | ISBN 9781641551250 (PDF format) |
 ISBN 9781641551274 (MOBI format)
Subjects: LCSH: Small houses. | Storage in the home. | Architecture, Domestic.
Classification: LCC TH4890 .K66 2019 | DDC 728/.37--dc23
LC record available at https://lccn.loc.gov/2019014742

Printed in the United States of America
10 9 8 7 6 5 4 3 2 1

IN LOVING MEMORY OF MARK WARMAN, GONE TOO SOON

ACKNOWLEDGMENTS

THANK YOU TO ALL OF THE ARCHITECTS, PHOTOGRAPHERS, AND HOMEOWNERS who took the time to talk with me and share their stories. You never fail to enlighten me and inspire me in each book that I write.

Peter Chapman is simply the most pleasant and professional editor a writer can be blessed to work with, and I thank him for his years of support and friendship. Taunton and the rest of the staff have always been a wonderful team to work with and offer great support.

My thanks to the architectural and construction community who generously continue to share information. I thank my immediate family, Rob, Alex and Jesse, my extended family, and dear friends, who continuously support my efforts and cheer me on throughout my research and writing.

This project was particularly rewarding as I've gone through the process of downsizing twice now. It has been life changing in many wonderful ways, and I can highly recommend living smaller.

CONTENTS

Groundswell House; photo by Acorn Art & Photography

INTRODUCTION

ACCORDING TO THE LATE GEORGE CARLIN, ALL YOU need in life is "a little place for your stuff." Unfortunately, that's just what keeps most people from downsizing to a smaller space: They have too much "stuff." It wasn't until I downsized myself that I experienced the terrific liberation that comes with living in a smaller space.

For 16 years my husband and I and our two children lived in a 6,800-sq.-ft. house in Greenwich, Connecticut. Over those years we entertained, did a good deal of cooking, and had a very active home. We hosted bridal showers, meetings, and other events. We had temporary guests for months on end and generally a full house.

The exterior detailing of the author's remodeled downsized house was retained to fit into the street of small cottages, while the windows were upgraded, the landscaping opened up, and a new driveway and garage added.
Photos by Randy O'Rourke

But our children moved on and the house became excessively large for just the two of us. The cost of having gardeners and pool service, keeping up with maintenance, and paying astronomical energy bills was too much. In addition, the house was on two and a half acres and was starting to feel very isolated with our empty nest. Although not far from town, it was still a trip to the grocery store and in a snowstorm, it felt like living in the Arctic. My husband and I knew it was time to move on.

As a family we'd accumulated lots of things that we thought we would keep forever—letters our children had written to us on open school nights, birthday cards, books, memorabilia, and so on.

They all seemed very precious at the time. When we made the decision to move out of our much-too-big house to a small, very cozy one, we quickly discovered that we had so many more things than we used or needed. Our furnishings were oversized and their design was from a different period of our lives. Figuring out what to do with it all was the biggest challenge. But we made the choice to free our life from all of the "stuff" and move on to a far more pared-down, happy life.

BEGINNING THE PURGE

For the several years our house was on the market, we went through a process of sporadic purging.

We built this Mediterranean-style house on two and a half acres. Although we enjoyed every bit of the space when our children were small, it started to become too big as they began to leave. In retrospect, now that we have lived "smaller," I think a smaller house would have been preferable during those years if it had been built according to the design parameters I've learned about since.
Photo by Simon Feldman Studio

Every so often we brought a bag of things to the recycling center, but when the time finally came to move, we realized that we'd accomplished almost nothing. We had closets full of clothes we didn't wear, oversized furniture that would never fit in a smaller house, nearly every small cooking appliance ever made, hundreds of books, memorabilia, and just lots and lots of stuff.

It took us too long to sell the house, but when it finally sold, we had just 40 days to unload everything we could not bring with us to our next home. Like most of the homeowners interviewed for this book, it became a process of purging and then purging again (and there is probably still another purge in our future!). The major purge started by getting rid of all the items we hadn't used, worn, read, or looked at in years; they had to be tossed. Moving into a much smaller space forced us to be very selective in deciding what to keep. We needed to look at our belongings in a different way. Do I need this? Will this ever be necessary for our future life? Have I touched this or looked at it in years?

Like many other people, we saved things for a variety of reasons: nostalgia, future need, changing sizes (maybe I'll lose 10 lb. and will be able to wear this again someday), and the hope that outdated clothing will come back in vogue. We offered our children their sweet little notes, handicrafts, and photos, but they had no interest in any of these things, so out they went. By the time we made the move, we had gotten rid of 90% of everything we had in our house. (People always ask us if we miss any of these things—it's a definite no.)

The first floor of the author's downsized house was opened up as a multipurpose space. The couch converts to a sleep sofa for overnight guests, the dining table doubles as a workspace, and the cabinets under the window benches provide additional storage. Sliding doors lead to a deck off the kitchen area, expanding the living space.

Photos by Randy O'Rourke

HOW TO MAKE A SMALL HOUSE FEEL BIG

Many of the downsizers I interviewed for this book were looking for certain well-defined aspects for their new home, including:

- Less square footage
- Lower energy costs
- Low-maintenance building materials and landscaping
- A master bedroom and bathroom on the main floor (especially popular with older homeowners)
- Universal design amenities so they can continue to live in their home later in life (aging in place)
- Lots of natural light
- Indoor/outdoor space to expand the living space
- Proximity to a town, slope, lake, or so on (which may not have been practical in thei previous home)

To live comfortably in a small house, there are many design features that help make the home feel comfortable and not so small. Many of these features are evident in most of the houses profiled in this book, designed by very creative and knowledgeable architects and designers:

- Minimal hallways
- Multipurpose rooms
- Open floor plan, allowing light to permeate the space
- Well-placed windows
- Built-in nooks
- Creative storage
- Smaller appliances
- High ceilings
- Light-colored cabinets and walls
- Open staircases
- Furnishings with added storage
- Dual-purpose furnishings
- Creative furnishing concepts, such as chairs hung on the wall, a drop-leaf table that opens, a dining table tucked under an island, a Murphy bed, and so on
- Rolling barn doors
- Pocket doors
- Access to outdoor space to extend the living space
- Porches and patios

As people age, more and more are living on fixed incomes and need to reduce their carrying charges. Moving to a smaller, more efficient home reduces energy costs, reduces the cost of construction, and if the house is built well, reduces maintenance costs. This small cottage is 280 sq. ft., located in Kennebunkport, Maine.

Photos by James R. Salomon

LIVING SMALLER

We moved to a 1,400-sq.-ft. house close to town, much more convenient to shopping, restaurants, movies, and so on. It was exciting to move to a smaller space, and, in retrospect, I wish we'd made the move years before. Like most of the homeowners featured in this book, life is happier for us in a smaller space rid of all that excess baggage and responsibility that comes with a large house. Now we focus more easily on keeping/buying just what we need. My husband and I keep a recycling bag in our bedroom. When we pull something out of the closet we don't think we'll wear any more, it goes in the bag—and eventually to the recycling center. If we buy something new, we look for something to get rid of. That way we never accumulate more than we need.

Luckily for us, we have an extra bedroom in our smaller house so when our son moved back home after graduating from college we had the space. And with a pullout couch in the living room and a futon in my office, there is room for our daughter and other guests as well. Having multipurpose/ flex space is ultimately much better than excessive space. And, of course, our maintenance and energy costs are a fraction of what they were previously when running our much larger house.

Having experienced the positive energy that comes with downsizing myself, it was gratifying to hear the same from many of the homeowners I interviewed. I'm hoping that the downsized homes these people have created will inspire others to consider all the possibilities that come with living in a smaller space. Many of the bright, comfortable, and flexible smaller spaces shown in these houses don't actually *feel* that small: "How to Make a Small House Feel Big" on the facing page gives some ideas on how to accomplish that.

WHO IS DOWNSIZING?

It's no surprise that the most obvious group of downsizers are empty nesters, part of the ever-expanding Baby Boomer generation. According to architect Jamie Wolf (who designed The Just Right House on p. 190), "Many people today are 'outgrowing' their too-big houses." Once the children are grown and moved away, the parents no longer need the space required when their families were growing. The choice becomes do we stay in the house with all its family memories or move to a more appropriately sized house, where every weekend is not taken up with maintenance and a hefty chunk of the budget goes toward the continual improvements required in the house?

There are many reasons empty nesters choose to downsize. Less space is generally the main reason, but they also want to reduce energy, mortgage, and maintenance expenses. A place with less to clean and a more intimate setting starts to look like a very good option. Boomers (as well as younger people) may decide to move to an area with a different climate or one where the cost of living is less. Some are moving back to the city, others are drawn to a rural location. They may desire or require a different configuration for the house. Downsizers may prefer a master bedroom on the main floor to avoid steps in their more senior years and may want/require Universal Design elements, such as grab bars in showers, easy-access bathtubs, barrier-free showers, extra-wide doorways, and limited steps, allowing them to continue living in their own home later in life. Some retirees (and young people) like to have the freedom to travel, which a smaller house may allow. One's home may be a stop-off destination between travels.

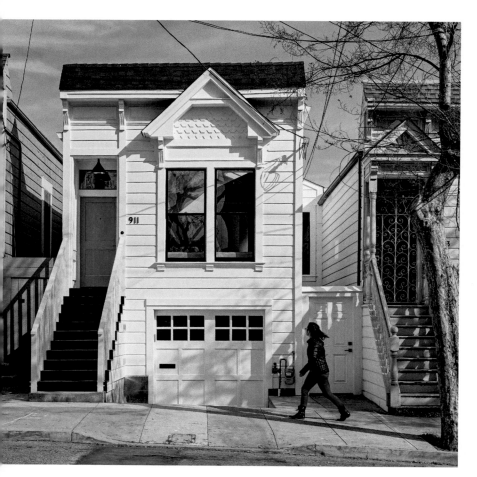

LEFT AND FACING PAGE: While wanting to live smaller, many people also choose to change the type of location: Some downsizers expressed a desire to live closer to town within walking distance of restaurants, stores, and entertainment, while others wanted to move to a more rural area closer to nature. Often people must sacrifice space to live close to town unless they have a generous budget. Shown here is the Dog Patch Pelton House, designed by architect Red Dot Studio.

Photos by Joe Fletcher Photography

A number of the downsized houses in this book were built to accommodate changes in family structure. For example, a couple of the houses are the result of divorced/widowed empty nesters, each with a house on their hands, coming together in one downsized abode (such as the Madison Passive house on p. 26). There are also those empty nesters now living alone after divorce or the death of a spouse in a much smaller house (such as the Morton House on p. 46).

Downsizing is not just for empty nesters

Many younger people are downsizing as well. They are getting tired of the costs associated with living in a large home, bogged down by the carrying charges for the house and the continuous upkeep. Both partners in a couple are likely working full time to pay the mortgage, heating, electricity, cable, water, and other bills without having time for each other or their children. They are spending all of their free time maintaining the house—the lawns, gardens, and all of the items in the house that need to be kept up. As a result, many families are tempted to find a more carefree way of life, choosing to downsize to a much smaller house or even a tiny house. They are more interested in using their extra funds for travel, entertainment, or sports rather than carrying large mortgage payments. They'd rather take biking trips than spend their weekends mowing the lawn and doing other chores that come with maintaining a large house.

A HAPPIER LIFE

Without exception, everyone I interviewed for this book was delighted to be downsizing. They universally acknowledged that they were happier. They used words such as "liberated," having rid themselves of all of the stuff or baggage that had loaded them down for years. Nobody said they missed any of the things that they got rid of. And none of the people said they missed the space (except perhaps when they would have liked to have large family gatherings).

Initially, some people said that their spouses got in their way in the smaller space, but they got used to the proximity and began to enjoy the closeness. Many of the houses were designed with private spaces, either with an outdoor area, a small office, or even a hallway lounge or desk, so everyone could have their own getaway space.

Without being bogged down by a lot of maintenance, people said they could enjoy other activities much more than in the past. Couples and families cooked together more often, went bike riding, pursued hobbies, traveled, and were able more often to do leisure activities when they downsized.

TOP LEFT: Designed by architects David J. Bailey and Stephanie Harrison-Bailey, this 665-sq.-ft. house in Ybor City, Florida, takes its inspiration from the shotgun-style houses of the historic neighborhood where the house is located. Built with steel-skinned structural insulated panels (SIPs) and helical piers for the foundation system, the house is very energy efficient.

TOP CENTER: Although small in square footage, the house has a roomy feel due to the open design, high ceilings, white walls and cabinetry, and well-placed windows. Paneling used throughout the interior adds more character than plain drywall.

TOP RIGHT: To take advantage of all the available space, a cozy dining area for two was created under the stairs.

Photos courtesy of Kathleen Bly

ENERGY EFFICIENCY AS A PRIORITY

Most of the homeowners featured in this book were very concerned about the environment, and reducing energy costs was a priority in their downsizing journey. They hired architects who were extremely knowledgeable about energy efficiency and worked with them to incorporate the most efficient systems and materials possible in their homes. Several of the houses were built to rigid energy standards such as Passive House (PH) and LEED (Leadership in Energy and Environmental Design) for Homes.

The houses were built with high-efficiency insulated windows and doors, extra insulation in the envelope of the house, and HVAC systems that are more efficient. Some of the houses incorporated solar energy, passive solar, and thermal mass in reducing the need for electricity. Most of the houses used LED and CFL lighting, high-efficiency appliances, and many other features to keep their energy needs to a minimum. These green features are listed for each house.

THE PROCESS OF DOWNSIZING

There is no doubt that getting rid of lots of possessions is a difficult task both emotionally and physically. Almost everyone interviewed for this book said that purging was more difficult than they anticipated. In actuality it takes a new mindset to downsize. One needs to be able to think: Do I need this? Will I ever use it or wear it? Does it give me pleasure? Is this something that is just collecting dust? Does this serve any purpose?

Most people go through several purges. The first items to be rid of are the obvious ones—those things in the basement or storage room you haven't looked at in years. The second purge usually comes when actual plans are in place to move to a smaller home. That is the time people have to start looking through their wardrobes for things they will never wear, furniture that is too big and is not needed, and nostalgia that is just taking up space. For some people this may be the end of the purge. For others, there is another purge that comes later. This includes the items still saved in storage or the basement until they can decide what to do with them. Most likely these items aren't needed or used and they can be tossed away later.

There is no sense paying to keep things in storage or paying to move them when they will likely be disposed of later. Children and relatives usually don't want these things and they may also be outdated. One homeowner told me his kids purposely avoided seeing him while he was downsizing so they didn't have to keep telling him they didn't want the things he was offering them!

There are many books that describe how to declutter your house of furnishings, clothing, books, and memorabilia. I will not get into these details here because of the wealth of information available on these topics. Rather, my hope is that readers will find in this book the inspiration to live in smaller spaces and learn from the design techniques used in these houses to make their own home comfortable and livable; that people will learn from all of the ways people have downsized and the techniques they have used to do so.

BUILDING OPTIONS

There are many ways to build a house—small or otherwise. It can be site built from the foundation up, prefabricated offsite and assembled in place, or an older house renovated to fit current needs. Those who have read my earlier books know my affinity for prefab construction, but the houses profiled here have been built using all three methods. And they are all beautiful, small, and well built—whichever method was used.

One particular category gaining in popularity is accessory dwelling units (ADUs), secondary living spaces attached or detached on the same lot as an existing primary single-family house. These can be an apartment over a garage, a basement apartment, or a smaller accessory structure on the same lot. ADUs are built for family members or for added income. Many municipalities are now allowing these units to be built with stipulations on how big they can be, who can live in them, and so on. (For more on ADUs, see the houses on pp. 66–71 and pp. 216–221.)

The Hillhurst Laneway House in Calgary, Canada, is an 850-sq.-ft. ADU (accessory dwelling unit) designed and built by Studio North. The grandparents live in the ADU while the parents and their small child live in the house beyond on the same property. It's an affordable option for grandparents who wish to age in place, live close to their family, but also maintain their independence.
Photo courtesy of Studio North

ABOVE: Inside the Hillhurst Laneway House, the open living space is on one floor, eliminating the need for stairs (save for a small loft space). The vaulted ceiling allows natural light from the dormers to flood into the ADU.
Photo courtesy of Studio North

LEFT: The bathroom has a curbless shower and fold-down seat, designed with aging in place in mind.
Photo courtesy of Studio North

Although all of the houses in this book are small (under 2,000 sq. ft.), they each include energy-saving technology, materials that require less maintenance, and upgraded materials that were perhaps not available when the owners built their previous larger home (such as quartz countertops, fiber cement siding, and standing-seam roofs).

Interestingly enough, the style of the downsized home is often considerably different than the family home the owners may have lived in for years. Some homeowners chose more modern styles, while others favored traditional ones. Downsizing gave all of the owners profiled here an opportunity to rethink their priorities, their styles, and their needs.

One significant trend I found is younger people planning for their golden years by building a house that they can someday retire to. They are building vacation homes in locations where they would like to live permanently when they become empty nesters. Some of these homes are in serene locations by lakes, the ocean, or the mountains or in more bustling areas close to town and activity. Some people build their house to use with their families and then move there permanently when they retire. And some younger people build houses with Universal Design features that can be their forever home, looking ahead toward all types of eventualities—older parents coming to live with them or becoming less mobile themselves.

HAPPY DOWNSIZING!

My hope in writing this book is that it will encourage the downsizer in you to make the transition from your too-big home to a more appropriate-sized one. Smaller does not mean less comfortable or less attractive. Several of the homeowners featured here said that their new small home more closely reflects their design aesthetic than the house they built many years earlier. In so many cases, these smaller homes have created a new and better beginning for the owners.

Used to living in a home with many big rooms and lots of space to move around, a lot of people can't imagine living in a small space. This book demonstrates that small houses can be comfortable, low maintenance, energy efficient, and beautiful. Consider the possibilities of downsizing for yourself!

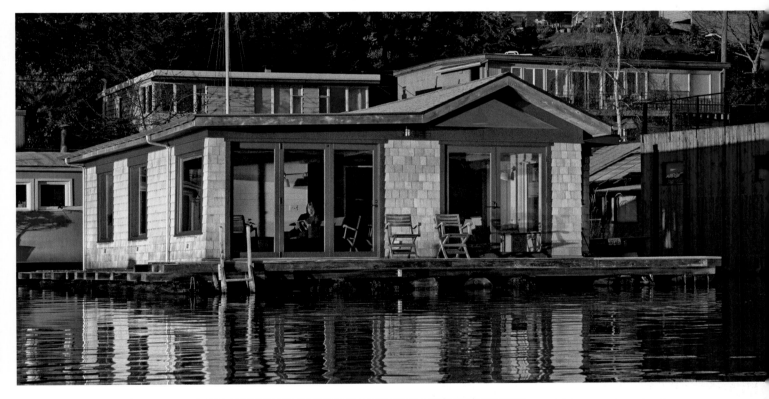

Living on a houseboat may not be for everyone, but some downsizers like the unique experience. Remodeled by Seattle-based SHKS Architects, the Portage Bay floating home is designed for future retirement.

Top photo by Dale Lang

Left photo by Benjamin Benschneider

EDMONDS HOUSE

CONSTRUCTION TYPE:
Panelized

**ARCHITECT/
MANUFACTURER:**
Stillwater Dwellings

PHOTOGRAPHER:
Jeff Amram Photography

LOCATION:
Edmonds, Wash.

SIZE:
1,900 sq. ft.

JOAN AND ERIC HAD LIVED IN A TWO-STORY, 3,200-sq.-ft. house in Seattle for 26 years. They were both born in Seattle and assumed they would live there forever. But as they got older, they became increasingly concerned about overcrowding and urban congestion, with all of the social problems that are typical of a large city. In short, they decided to find a smaller, quieter community close to Seattle that offered a friendly, laid-back lifestyle. They also sought a community where they could walk to stores, restaurants, and cultural events without having to drive.

DOWNSIZING TO A MORE APPROPRIATE HOUSE

Another consideration in making the move was that their house was becoming too big for them to maintain, and they found they were not using all the space they had. It was time to relocate to a house that was better suited to their current and future needs. And that, of course, meant downsizing. Joan and Eric had many more items than they needed or wanted, some of which had been passed down to them from parents and grandparents. Although these items had some sentimental value, it felt wonderful to let it all go.

It was easier for Joan to downsize than it was for Eric. She defines herself as a minimalist in terms of possessions and had lived on a boat for 12 years many years ago (giving away most of her belongings to do so). She finds it easier to let go of stuff than Eric and got rid of most of her professional work clothes soon after she retired. As well as her clothes, books, assorted knickknacks, and other household items went to charity. Her sister and neighbors took some things, and then she hired a company to sell everything else, except for a few pieces of furniture and some of their favorite artwork. Getting rid of so much while still living in their old house made the move to the new house much easier.

FINDING EDMONDS

Joan and Eric found their perfect community 20 minutes north of Seattle in the beautiful town of Edmonds—a welcoming beach town with a very active arts scene. And within that town they found a teardown property in a perfect location just a block from the water and three blocks from the commuter train that goes to downtown Seattle and the state ferry.

Although the building site was a small infill lot, the design of the house focused on creating an intimate indoor/outdoor space through the use of large sliding-glass doors and a complete wall of southeast-facing glass. They built a studio for Joan's artwork and office, situated in the backyard

The environmental impact of the house was a significant consideration in the design. High insulation values in the roof, walls, and floors maintain high-energy performance. In addition, the exterior walls are concrete panels with a standing-seam roof for low maintenance.

The house has an open plan with easy circulation between kitchen, living, and dining room areas. Most of the furnishings were bought new to fit with the owners' new home.

PANELIZED CONSTRUCTION

Panelized construction is a type of prefabrication that uses panels premade in a factory and then assembled on a foundation. There are numerous advantages to this type of construction. Production and installation of the panels is much faster than on-site construction, making the house weathertight more quickly; the panels are produced in a protected environment, which avoids damage from the elements, creates less disturbance to the neighborhood, and generates far less waste. Flooring, wall, and roofing components can be used to build any style home. For more information about the panelized system used for the Edmonds house, go to stillwaterdwellings.com.

so it blocked the line of site from neighboring homes. They also put in two privacy screens and planted trees that would block the views of other neighbors. They chose Stillwater to build their house because they were interested in panelized, minimalist construction (see sidebar, left) and liked the contemporary open designs Stillwater offered.

AGING IN PLACE

Joan and Eric both worked in healthcare and had witnessed first-hand people being forced into apartments or long-term care facilities because their homes were no longer safe for them to return to. Although they are still fit and healthy, they wanted to avoid that happening to them by building a home that was as ADA-compliant as possible, allowing them to age in place gracefully.

WIDE HALLWAYS AND DOORWAYS

Wide hallways and doorways are essential in an ADA (Americans with Disabilities Act)-compliant house. These accommodations make it possible to maneuver a wheelchair or scooter if this becomes necessary at some point in life. Owners Joan and Eric requested their home be built ADA-compliant to accommodate aging in place.

According to ADA requirements, the minimum width of a hallway for a wheelchair is 48 in. and for a doorway, 36 in. Obviously it is better to plan for wider hallways before the house is built rather than after it is constructed. For more information about ADA Standards for Accessible Design, check out the website: ada.gov/2010ADAstandards_index.htm.

Their new house had to be on one level with wide hallways and door openings as well as curbless showers. They also selected light fixtures that were ADA-compliant, tile that was slip resistant, and sinks with depths recommended for wheelchair accessibility. At the same time, Joan and Eric wanted to have a beautiful house that did not look like it was built for aging or disabilities but that would be suitable if the need ever arose. Not only was the house designed for the owners to age in place but also for their rescue dog and cat. The architect designed a dog/cat door in the mudroom/laundry area that has a little ramp to their door, so their pets can age in place as well.

Joan and Eric recommend making all aging-in-place requests in the design stage of the construction, particularly with a prefab house, where all of the design is completed and finished in advance. Making these changes on a house that is set becomes more challenging. They discovered that

DOWNSIZING FEATURES

- One-floor living
- Wide hallways and door openings
- Barrier-free shower, curb-less doors to outside
- Walkable community

GREEN FEATURES

- Infill lot
- Low-maintenance materials
- Concrete panel siding
- Standing-seam roof

GARAGE

MUDROOM

GUEST/OFFICE

BEDROOM

KITCHEN

LIVING ROOM

DINING ROOM

MASTER BEDROOM

PATIO

Operable windows and door, as well as the clerestory windows above, bring in a good deal of light and provide natural ventilation. The master bedroom opens onto a private patio.

the hard way when they had to make some changes after they moved in. They replaced one door with a barn door, to provide more room in the bathroom to move around, and changed another bathroom door to swing out instead of in. They also removed the planned soaking tub because the master bath design did not provide adequate turning radius for a wheelchair or adequate turn space.

A PROVEN CONCEPT

The first guest to stay in the house was a young (50ish) friend who had fallen and broken her hip while bicycling. Her surgeon wanted her to go to a rehabilitation facility for six weeks, but Joan suggested she stay at their house instead. Their bathroom and shower easily accommodated her wheelchair and subsequent walker. The extra-wide hallways and doorways made it easy for her to navigate the house and be able to go outside to use the patio. The house clearly not only works for the owners but for their friends as well.

ABOVE: The rear of the house is mostly glass, with operable doors and windows and clerestory windows high on the walls. This expands the feeling of spaciousness in the house, and the patios provide another area for sitting and relaxing. All of the door openings are curbless—ideal for aging in place and safety in general.

LEFT: The deep overhangs, typical of Stillwater Dwellings designs, protect the house from the elements and help limit the summer heat gain while allowing the sun to warm the house when it is lower in the sky during the colder months.

NEW STREET HOUSE

CONSTRUCTION TYPE:
Site Built

ARCHITECT:
Cooter Ramsey, Allison
Ramsey Architects

PHOTOGRAPHER:
Sandy Dimke

LOCATION:
Beaufort, S.C.

SIZE:
1,906 sq. ft.

ANDY AND NANCY LIVED IN A 3,550-SQ.-FT. HOME in Beaufort for 12 years before they decided it was time to downsize. Even though the house wasn't excessively large, it had lots of "pieces and parts" that had to be cleaned and maintained, such as a pool, a boat lift, a dock, and a large yard. They were getting tired of the upkeep. In downsizing they wanted to go smaller, spend less time and money maintaining everything, and devote more time to having fun and traveling. They also wanted the house to be more energy efficient and within walking distance of downtown.

THE NEW HOME

Nancy and Andy found their happy place when they built their new home on New Street in the historic district of downtown Beaufort. Maintenance is now minimal: Instead of the weeks that it used to take them to get the yard in shape for spring, it's now done in just a weekend. They don't have grass to mow or a pool to maintain, making it easier for them to go out of town. They still have lots of plants, but they now have a sprinkler system or the dog sitter to water them.

While their new home is smaller, they didn't have to compromise on storage space, which was a priority in the design. The new kitchen has more cabinet space than the previous kitchen and a larger pantry—and then there's the walk-in attic, which has ample space for Christmas and other seasonal decorations. Nancy says that by having lots of storage space, the house is devoid of clutter.

The couple opted to build the house a foot higher than what the National Flood Program required. This not only gave them a discount on their flood insurance but it also allows them to feel more secure in the house and provides the added bonus of extra storage space under the house. Although the raised porch creates extra steps up to the house, Andy appreciates the exercise as an opportunity to stay in shape. It also provides security against package thieves. For even more security, they have a camera on the front and back porches. (Knowing that Andy is an insurance agent makes his concern a bit more understandable.)

ADJUSTING TO A SMALLER HOME

While Nancy and Andy were downsizing, a friend asked Nancy if she would regret not having space for all of the kids to stay with them at the same time. Nancy assured her that this might only be the case two nights a year, pointing out that it hardly makes sense to maintain a large home for something that happens so infrequently. And when the occasional

Most houses in the Beaufort Historic District, like this one, have front porches, which make casual meetings with neighbors effortless. The fiber cement board siding is low maintenance and long lasting. The porch is also 1 foot higher than the required flood zone requirement to avoid flood and insurance issues.

ABOVE AND RIGHT: Tall double-hung windows admit a good deal of light. The kitchen includes white quartz countertops, a coffee bar, and a serving/eating peninsula, with a wine cooler and second beverage cooler below it. An undercounter lighting and power system with USB charger ports minimizes the number of receptacles along the backsplash.

need arises, Nancy says, "there is a little hotel just down the street if we ever need more space. (And they do the sheets)."

At first it was an adjustment for Nancy and Andy living in a smaller house, getting in each other's way. But with time, they adapted and began to enjoy the coziness of their new home. They miss having a study/media room and the ability to entertain large groups of family and friends, but enjoy living a more carefree life. One of the benefits of moving to this smaller house has been the couple's involvement in neighborhood activities. Because they are able to walk to their neighbors, they can be a lot more spontaneous since they don't have to deal with traffic or finding a parking place.

For Andy, one of the best things about the house is living in a true urban historic neighborhood with a historic church across the street and a terrific chocolatier nearby. He and Nancy enjoy walking to town and having great friendly neighbors. With minimal upkeep, low utility bills, and the freedom to travel, downsizing to the house on New Street was the ideal move.

LIGHT WALLS FOR SMALL ROOMS

Dark colors tend to absorb light, which makes a room appear smaller than it is. Light colors, particularly white, reflect light and make rooms look larger. Continuous color throughout a room also tends to make a room look larger; painting an accent wall will break up the continuity and may make it look smaller. White, pastels, and neutrals are often recommended for small rooms. The same is true for the ceilings and floorings: light colors make rooms appear larger and brighter. Color is a matter of personal choice, so if you like a dark room, go for it—but be aware it may make the room claustrophobic, particularly if there aren't many windows.

Built-ins in the living room provide much-needed storage in a smaller house. The light walls help to make this house appear larger than it is.

Nancy's sewing room occupies one of the two rooms on the second floor. The wide-board light-colored French oak engineered flooring used here and throughout most of the house is dimensionally stable, durable, and reasonably priced.

A rimless shower was included in the first-floor master bathroom for safety and accessibility. The ample walk-in closet beyond the bathroom provides excellent storage.

DOWNSIZING FEATURES
- Barrier-free shower
- Low-maintenance landscaping
- High ceilings
- Natural lighting
- Light-colored walls
- Lots of storage

GREEN FEATURES
- ENERGY STAR appliances
- Low-flow faucets and showerheads
- Spray foam insulation
- Water purification system

BACK PORCH

MASTER BEDROOM

KITCHEN

BEDROOM

DINING ROOM

LIVING ROOM

BEDROOM

FRONT PORCH

SECOND FLOOR

FIRST FLOOR

ABOVE LEFT: The entrance from the back porch is via the mudroom and laundry area. Ample seating, storage, and coat hooks—as well as a porcelain wood finish floor and sliding door into the kitchen—make this space perfect for transitioning from the outside into the house. It also serves as the dogs' dedicated sleeping area.

ABOVE RIGHT: A wall of windows in the master bedroom floods the room with light and a view to the backyard over the porch. The ceiling fan allows the couple to minimize use of the air-conditioning system.

LEFT: At the back of the house, a patio with pergola, wood-fired oven, seating area, and brick sitting wall provides a roomy space for entertaining, more than compensating for the downsized interior.

BLUE PORCH CEILINGS

What started out as a Southern tradition, blue ceilings on porches have become a trend across the country. "Haint" blue is a pale shade of blue that is traditionally used because it was believed to keep away evil spirits. (According to the Urban Dictionary, haint is a southern colloquialism,

defined as ghost, apparition, lost soul.) Other theories for painting the ceiling blue are that it brings good luck, extends the daylight, or fools wasps and spiders into believing the ceiling is the sky. Today, a variety of blue shades are used for porch ceilings, including aqua, periwinkle, and teal.

MADISON PASSIVE

CONSTRUCTION TYPE:
Site Built

ARCHITECT:
Tessa Smith, Artisans Group

PHOTOGRAPHER:
Poppi Photography

LOCATION:
Olympia, Wash.

SIZE:
1,462 sq. ft.

CERTIFICATION:
Passive House Certified

JEFF SOLD HIS 3,500-SQ.-FT. HOUSE AFTER HIS WIFE passed away. It was the house he had lived in for 27 years and where he had raised his children. He began to feel overwhelmed by the home because of its excess space and its personal history. He decided to sell the house and keep whatever he could move into a POD storage container and either sell or give away the rest. Jeff wanted to live in downtown Olympia but found that the available apartments and condos didn't provide space for his biking lifestyle.

Sue raised her children in south central California and decided to visit Olympia on the advice of a friend. She moved to Olympia, bought a newer home around 1,700 sq. ft., but found it to be incredibly inefficient. Its design seemed to stifle neighbor interaction while simultaneously getting too hot in the summer and too cold in the winter. She then downsized to a 900-sq.-ft. home that was much more energy efficient but wasn't quite large enough to support her biking and social lifestyle.

When Jeff got together with Sue they decided they wanted the opportunity to live an urban lifestyle without an enormous footprint. Together, they found a small (20-ft. by 60-ft.) empty lot just on the edge of downtown. When they were ready to build, Artisans Group (AG) designed the house for these two active adults—a house where they could live in a thriving community, enjoy life, even as they grow older, and foster their health and happiness as they age.

AGING-IN-PLACE FEATURES, HIDDEN IN PLAIN SIGHT
Although the couple is very active now, they designed their house to be livable for the rest of their lives. With a single story, wide hallways, a tiled rimless shower, and a built-in dining nook that can be easily accessed by a wheelchair, the house is well equipped to be their forever home. They recognize and are planning for happiness as life happens. "A home design that recognizes its inhabitants will age, and that age will affect mobility, means that they can enjoy their home for longer, not be angry at the difficulties and limitations," architect Tessa Smith explains.

BUILDING THEIR DREAM HOME
Sue and Jeff saw all of their collections of excess stuff as more of a burden than a benefit. So they had the house designed with much less space than they had previously, with durability and performance built in. They wanted less maintenance, healthier air, and a drastically smaller carbon

The couple chose this corner lot in the heart of Olympia because of the established neighborhood and proximity to downtown. With its raised stoop and welcoming front porch, the house provides engagement with neighborhood passersby while maintaining privacy due to carefully placed windows and clerestories.

ABOVE: The kitchen is both clean and modern but welcoming, with warm wood touches in the ceiling and cabinetry. Plentiful storage allows countertops to be kept bare, with lots of space for food preparation. The cable lighting across the kitchen provides lowered task lighting when the couple needs it.

LEFT: Although the owners love modern architecture, they wanted a warm Pacific Northwest feeling, something more accessible and friendly than austere and white. The ceiling is tongue-and-groove 4-in. clear cedar stained to match the fir doors and the exterior soffit, providing visual continuity from inside out or outside in.

FACING PAGE TOP AND BOTTOM: The breakfast nook at the edge of the kitchen is graced by a custom-made table, built according to the architect's design. The floors are polished unstained concrete with radiant heating in the slab. The 14-ft. ceilings help to bring plenty of sunlight into the house.

footprint than a typical code-built, insulated and sealed home. They wanted also to make sure that they had adequate storage space for the items they brought with them.

Sue and Jeff knew of Artisans Group from touring one of their first passive houses. After meeting with Tessa they knew this was the right firm for what they were hoping to build. They liked their designs, and given Sue's earlier experience with inefficient homes, she knew she wanted one that was highly energy efficient. Jeff also was very interested in building the house using minimal energy. With AG's experience with passive houses, she and Jeff knew they would get the house they dreamed of.

According to Tessa, "Building a passive house is always a challenge, but we've developed design techniques that are tried-and-true, and Madison Passive is a study in pulling those learned lessons together into this new energy-efficient home. Madison Passive is a heartening tale for future home construction because it's proof that a passive house can work on small infill lots, that you can have a beautiful and extremely energy-efficient home; they're not mutually exclusive."

This utility/bike storage room provides ample storage space for the couple's many bicycles, outerwear and shoes, the washer/dryer, and the mechanicals.

DOWNSIZING FEATURES
- Single story
- Wide hallways
- Barrier-free shower
- Built-in dining nook
- High ceilings
- Ample storage

GREEN FEATURES
- LED lights
- Heat recovery ventilator (HRV)
- ENERGY STAR appliances
- Natural daylighting
- Superinsulation
- Concrete floors

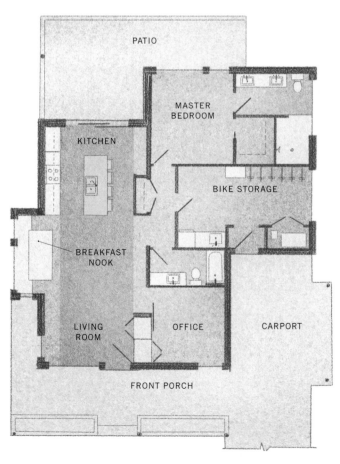

PATIO

MASTER BEDROOM

KITCHEN

BIKE STORAGE

BREAKFAST NOOK

LIVING ROOM

OFFICE

CARPORT

FRONT PORCH

The concrete wall that frames the back patio created a way to cut into the site's steep slope. In addition to having an architectural quality that matches the rectilinear aspects of this home, the wall also has a practical function of being low enough to sit on, or to set drinks or food plates on when hosting. It also creates a nice enclosed privacy buffer, particularly as the landscaping matures.

STORAGE: AN IMPORTANT ASPECT OF SMALL HOUSES

One of the biggest obstacles homeowners face when downsizing is finding enough storage space for the things that have made the cut and are moving to the new house. When the architect is designing the house it is essential that adequate storage be built into the plan.

This house, though small, has ample storage space. There are cabinets in almost every room—although hidden behind what looks like beautiful wood paneling. Particularly if

there is no basement or storage room in the house, cabinets must be built into walls or any excess space found around the house. Furniture with built-in storage is also ideal. As an example of clever storage, the hanging rack for bicycles in the Madison Passive holds several bikes without taking up much space. The cabinets give Sue and Jeff plenty of places to store all of their possessions, maintaining a clean and modern appearance.

GROUNDSWELL HOUSE

CONSTRUCTION TYPE:
Site Built

ARCHITECT:
Solterre Design

PHOTOGRAPHER:
Adam Cornick,
Acorn Art & Photography

LOCATION:
Cow Bay, Nova Scotia,
Canada

SIZE:
1,920 sq. ft.

AN IMPORTANT ASPECT OF SUCCESSFUL DOWNSIZING is having flexible spaces that can accommodate sleepovers. When Karen and Warren's three adult children and their partners are all home, everyone is inclined to fight over which space they will use. The most popular space is the four-season screened porch/sunroom where they can wake up the next morning to bright sunshine streaming in. The other sleeping option is the television room where the walls are all black, with a wood ceiling and a big rolling barn door. They say it is "like sleeping in a cave, perfect for the night owls watching TV till the late hours." There is also a secret loft (above the en suite bathroom in the bedroom wing), where future grandchildren will have a great time. Ironically, the one place Karen and Warren usually can't get anyone to sleep is the spare bedroom.

Karen and Warren had owned property in Cow Bay for 12 years before deciding to build a house on the shore. They previously lived in nearby Cole Harbour in a 2,400-sq.-ft. house on a two-acre property with lots of trees but no view of the ocean. Their new home in Cow Bay is steps from the water with fantastic views of the bluff and ocean. One of the owners is a keen surfer so proximity and views of the local surf breaks were key in their decision to downsize to this location. Wildlife abounds right outside their windows with deer, eagles, hawks, pheasants, and various species of songbirds, porcupines, raccoons, and foxes.

In addition to the proximity to the water and beautiful views, there are additional advantages to this new location. Cow Bay is a great community, with a community hall just down the road from the couple's property that hosts holiday and musical events featuring local artists. Several friends have also moved to this area for all of its attractions.

The other important consideration was building a smaller, more energy-efficient home to help insulate Karen and Warren from any future rises in energy costs. The home is planned to be net-zero energy with a photovoltaic array offsetting their energy use. Reduced maintenance time was also a requirement, allowing the couple more time to do the things they most enjoy.

DOWNSIZING COMFORTABLY

Having to downsize was not a big issue for Karen and Warren. They already lived an "edited beachy lifestyle and had a pared-down home—although not minimalist." They try to live a life that avoids being too consumer oriented in a disposable society. It probably helped that they'd just spent two years living in a 1,200-sq.-ft. two-level three-bedroom house in the heart of Dartmouth on busy Portland Street while the house was being

The gable roof rises higher in the more public spaces to take advantage of the view with larger windows and is lower in the smaller-windowed bedroom area. The materials are low maintenance, including the standing-seam aluminum roof, locally harvested and manufactured *Shou Sugi Ban* wood, and spruce shiplap siding. Orange trim around the windows adds a warm pop of color.

The kitchen is open to the living and dining areas, with peninsula islands separating the space on either side. Kitchen cabinets are hardwood and stained plywood. The rolling barn door on the back side opens onto a cozy television room.

THERMAL MASS

Thermal mass is a solid or a liquid material that can absorb and store warmth and coolness until it is needed. High-density materials such as concrete, brick, and stone have the ability to store and release energy back into a living space, at a delayed rate. Proper placement of these materials in floors, interior walls made of adobe or brick, or a large stone or brick fireplace will increase the amount of thermal mass in the home and make it more energy efficient.

During the summer, heat is absorbed in the cooler surfaces of the home, which keeps the space comfortable and reduces the need for air conditioning. In winter, the same thermal mass materials can store heat from the sun and release it at night when the room's air temperature falls. This is the concept that makes the concrete flooring in this house most effective.

built. So the new one-level house felt like quite the upgrade.

The new house has one less bedroom, and each of the rooms is a bit smaller than the couple had in their previous Cole Harbour home. Even though most spaces are a bit smaller, all their furniture from their previous house fit, requiring them to eliminate furniture from just one bedroom. The couple also wanted the space to be flexible so they could switch rooms around, such as between the dining area and the living room. They say this keeps the house feeling new. Flex space was an important feature, so the smaller spaces could be well used, from sleeping their adult children to doing craft projects.

DESIGNING A FOREVER HOUSE

The couple asked Solterre Design to create a plan with lots of open space, high vaulted ceilings, and expansive windows to bring in lots of light and natural ventilation. They also wanted multiple outdoor spaces that would make the house feel larger than it actually is.

The screened porch/sunroom was designed as an additional living area that was cost-effective to build with less insulation and less expensive

ABOVE: A picture window and glass door in the living area bring in lots of natural light and solar energy, captured by the concrete floor's thermal mass. A woodstove keeps the couple warm on the coldest days.

RIGHT: The master bedroom features a wall of random-width birch plank cladding and a ceiling fan overhead.

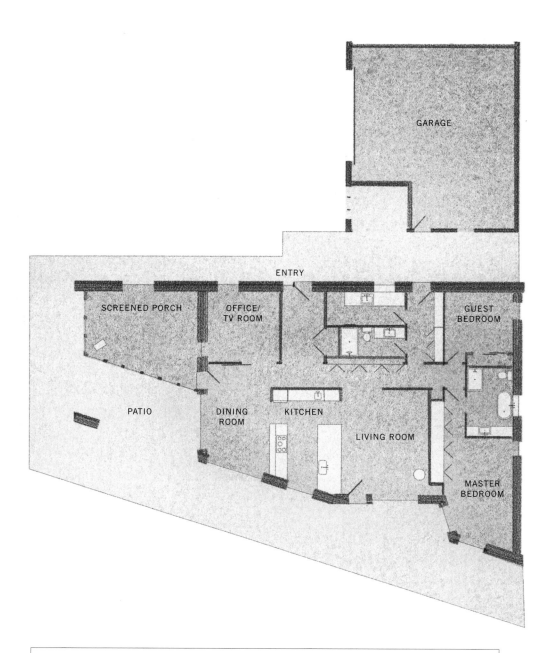

GARAGE

ENTRY

SCREENED PORCH

OFFICE/
TV ROOM

GUEST
BEDROOM

PATIO

DINING
ROOM

KITCHEN

LIVING ROOM

MASTER
BEDROOM

DOWNSIZING FEATURES
- One-floor living
- Walk-in shower
- Flex room
- Creative storage space
- Three-season porch
- Multiple outdoor spaces
- Vaulted ceilings

GREEN FEATURES
- Daylighting
- Optimal solar orientation
- Triple-glazed windows
- Photovoltaic (PV) system
- Recycled materials
- Heat pump hot-water heater
- High-efficiency plumbing fixtures
- Ceiling fans
- Concrete floors
- Superinsulation
- 0.53 ACH at 50 pascals

The dining area is bathed in light from both full and clerestory windows. The large island in the kitchen and 8-ft. dining table function as a workspace for Karen and the kids, as well as an eating area.

three-season windows. To make it a four-season room, they later decided to add a woodstove.

With the house on one level, it will be possible for the couple to age in place and possibly have their elderly parents move in someday. With a multipurpose flex room off the dining room, they have an office, a television viewing room, and an extra guest room if needed. Moving some storage to an unheated space in the garage loft reduced the need for more conditioned interior storage in the house.

REACHING NET ZERO

The house was designed effectively to meet the net-zero efficiency target. Ground-mounted solar panels separate from the house provide all of the electricity needed. Concrete floors with thermal mass (see sidebar, p. 34) maintain the heat and cool and release it when it is needed. The expansive windows provide lots of natural light, which helps to warm the floors.

Warren tallied up his electricity bills for the first year living in the house, and with the net-metered photovoltaic (PV) system, he found that they spent just $7 on electricity—which means that the photovoltaic solar array produced all but $7 of electricity that the house used in one year. The house was planned to be net-zero energy, but architect David Gallagher says, "It is great to get this confirmation after a year of use. Because the home is electrically heated and cooled, this accounts for all the utility bills for the home excepting a small amount for firewood." It is reassuring for the owners to know that they will have such low operating costs for their long future in their dream home.

ABOVE: Birch plank cladding adds a warm touch to the angular modern design of the screened porch/sunroom. The small woodstove and three-season windows (screens with an acrylic cover) mean that the space can be used year round.

LEFT: The house is situated on the Atlantic coast, with views of the ocean. Ground-mounted solar panels provide all of the electricity needed for the house.

FACING PAGE TOP: A sheltered courtyard is formed by the garage and house, buffering winter winds. A breezeway connects the house and garage. Both the garage and front doors are a welcoming orange, like the trim around the windows.

SHOU SUGI BAN

Shou Sugi Ban (which translates as "the burning of Japanese cypress") is a traditional Japanese technique of charring wood to make it more rot and insect resistant. A number of woods can be treated this way, including spruce, which was used on the exterior of this home.

There are a variety of ways to create the charred-wood effect. One of the original processes involves binding three boards together in a triangular tube and then burning the wood from the inside just deep enough to get the black-silver finish. The wood is sometimes left in that charred state or finished with oil to bring out the gray, silver, or other tones. This charring process preserves the wood, eliminates the sap in the wood, and makes it resistant to fire, rot, and pests. The wood used for this house was produced in a workshop with an automatic feeder and torch. For further information, visit shousugiban.com.

HOUSE ON WALDEN POND

CONSTRUCTION TYPE:
Post and Beam/
Panelized

**DESIGNER/
MANUFACTURER/
BUILDER:**
Yankee Barn Homes

PHOTOGRAPHER:
Bob Gothard

LOCATION:
Concord, Mass.

SIZE:
1,467 sq. ft.

AFTER MANY YEARS IN THEIR 2,500-SQ.-FT. HOUSE on the southern side of Concord, Mass., Dugie and John Thompson were ready for their next move, a home to retire to. Downsizing was definitely high on their wish list, as a smaller house would translate to lower taxes, lower utility costs, and less maintenance. They also wanted a two-car garage, something their current home lacked, and a home that would allow them to entertain frequently and with ease.

As you'll see repeatedly throughout this book, disposing of a lifetime of accumulated possessions is one of the biggest challenges of downsizing. For Dugie and John, it was even more difficult than they'd anticipated, and ultimately they hired a home clean-up specialist to help them with this onerous task.

BUILDING WITH YANKEE BARN HOMES

The couple had lived in a timber-frame home previously, so the choice of timbered construction was an easy one: it was both familiar and comfortable. Dugie and John chose Yankee Barn Homes (YBH) because of its insulated panelized system and energy-efficient shell package. This combined efficiency allows for comfortable living with reduced costs—a key element for their choice to downsize. Post-and-beam construction, which YBH specializes in, also requires fewer interior support walls than typical stick-frame construction, allowing dynamic interior volumes of space and an abundance of natural light. With fewer support walls, the house has a very open feeling. Dugie and John have all the room they need, in a relatively compact footprint.

And why Walden Pond? The area was particularly meaningful for Dugie, because Walden Pond and Fairhaven Woods were her playground growing up (she and her brother learned to swim in Walden Pond). Her family house is about $1/4$ mile from their new home, and Thoreau, author of *Walden,* and the other Concord transcendentalists used to picnic on the "Cliffs" located on their family land.

BUILDING A FOREVER HOME

Because Dugie and John envision the house as their forever home, it was designed for the future eventualities of aging. The house features a first-floor master bedroom and an adjoining bathroom with curbless shower and oversized shower door as well as a comfort-height toilet. Door frames throughout are sized to accommodate wheelchair access should it ever be needed. An upstairs bedroom and bathroom can be used by visiting family and friends.

This post-and-beam house sits on a beautiful wooded 3.35-acre hillside overlooking the state park that surrounds Walden Pond. Exterior materials include clear eastern cedar shingles, black framed windows, and an asphalt shingle roof.

Dugie and John miss their old house and the memories created there, but they love their new home with its familiar timber structure. As Dugie says, "Being among the trees of the Walden Pond area, there is a wonderful feel to the timbers and the open spaces of our home that fits in so well with the landscape." She and her husband can't wait to make new memories here.

The open plan is anchored by the kitchen, which has cedar plank ceiling boards, ceramic subway tile walls, painted Shaker panel cabinets, and engineered-quartz countertops. Floors are rift- and quartersawn reclaimed white oak. In the absence of a dedicated dining room, Dugie and John eat at the raised, full-length verde marble dining counter behind the kitchen countertop.

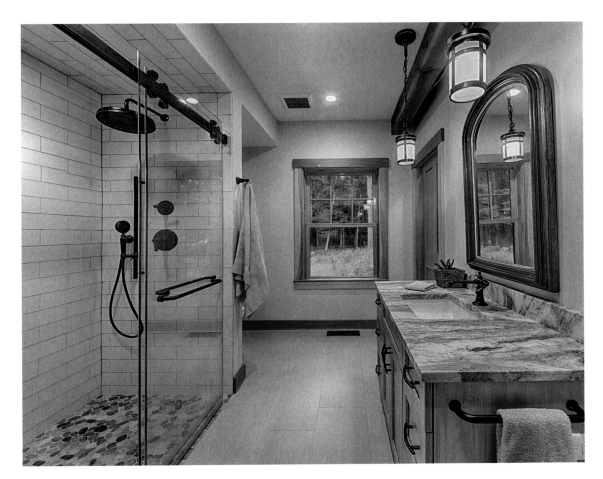

The master bathroom continues the home's theme of warm woods and ceramic tile. Dark metal hardware accents on plumbing fittings, the shower door, and lighting contribute to an industrial yet handmade feel. The rimless shower with oversize door was designed with accessibility in mind.

ON-DEMAND HOT WATER

When people are downsizing, saving on energy is a major priority, not only reducing space but also utility costs. On-demand hot water (in the form of tankless water heaters) is one way of lowering energy costs. These heaters provide hot water only when you want it, which means not wasting energy heating water when you don't need it. Cold water circulates through a series of coils, which are directly heated by gas burners or electric coils. The unit goes on only when you turn on the hot-water faucet.

On-demand water heaters provide hot water at a rate of 2 to 5 gal. per minute, depend-ing on the model. Gas-fired on-demand water heaters produce higher flow rates than the electric ones. Some houses may require a second unit if hot-water demands are great. Some units provide enough hot water only for a tub or washing machine at one time; others can supply enough for multiple simultane-ous needs. These units generally cost more than a typical 40-gal. water heater, but they usually have longer warranties, last longer, and save money on energy. To learn more, visit the Department of Energy Efficiency and Renewable Energy website at eere.energy.gov.

DOWNSIZING FEATURES

- First-floor master suite
- Daylighting
- High ceilings
- Barrier-free shower
- Minimal hallways
- Multiple pocket doors

GREEN FEATURES

- Engineered-quartz countertop
- Locally sourced material
- Low-flow water fixtures
- Sustainable Forestry Initiative (SFI)-certified lumber
- Reclaimed antique hard pine (kitchen) and cedar (living room)
- Passive solar
- Advanced framing
- ENERGY STAR-rated appliances
- ENERGY STAR-rated windows and doors
- High-efficiency propane boiler
- On-demand hot water (tankless water heater)
- High-efficiency insulation
- Insulated joists and sill plates

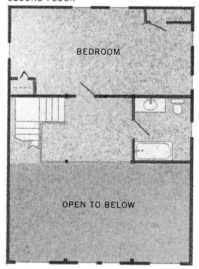

SECOND FLOOR

BEDROOM

OPEN TO BELOW

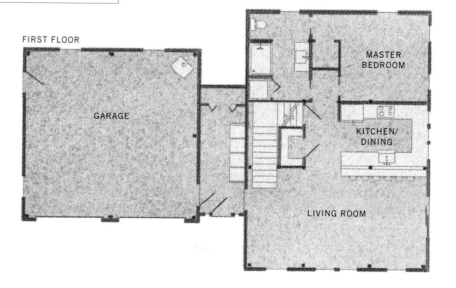

FIRST FLOOR

GARAGE

MASTER BEDROOM

KITCHEN/ DINING

LIVING ROOM

POST AND BEAM VS. TIMBER FRAME

People often use these two terms interchangeably because the construction styles both feature fully exposed timbers in the interior of the house. But there are some minor differences in the two types of construction, the main one being the type of joinery used. Post-and-beam construction typically uses hidden fasteners or decorative metal braces. Timber-frame construction requires a type of joinery called mortise and tenon, secured by wooden pegs. The precision necessary to cut the mortise and tenon can be very labor intensive, adding to the cost of timber-frame construction.

The other difference in the two types of construction is the type of beams used. Post-and-beam construction can include laminated engineered wood products or solid beams. Timber frames are usually constructed only with solid beams.

The beauty of this post-and-beam structure, with its dramatic timber framing, shines from the second floor loft, where a pair of ceiling fans complements the timber textures.

Yankee Barn Homes frames are precut, sanded, and stained in their New Hampshire facility prior to site delivery. The post-and-beam frame structure is then raised at the site, along with the panelized wall and roof. The double-high ceilings and double row of windows in the great room create a light-filled airy feel.

MORTON HOUSE

CONSTRUCTION TYPE:
Site Built

ARCHITECT:
Hicks Stone,
Stone Architecture

BUILDER:
Owner

PHOTOGRAPHER:
Randy O'Rourke

LOCATION:
Sharon, Conn.

SIZE:
1,005 sq. ft.

AFTER GETTING DIVORCED, TOM MORTON DECIDED he wanted to build a house for himself that would be minimal, environmentally friendly, and unique. He wanted it to be rustic yet modern, have a small footprint but feel open, be simple but high functioning, and most of all be sustainable. Tom's friend, German Passive House (PH)–certified architect Hicks Stone, helped him with the land selection and site of the house as well as its design and layout: a simple two-room structure with a living, dining, and kitchen area and a bedroom with an en suite bathroom. Given Hicks's experience, Tom knew he would get the energy-efficient house he was envisioning.

Tom had had some experience in the building trades, so he decided to pull together a crew and build the house himself. He formed a small construction company and hired Bernie Plonski, a 70-year-old, highly experienced carpenter/contractor. The house was completed in a year. Tom says Bernie understood exactly what he was trying to achieve and could build almost anything (and on budget). At his age, Bernie appreciated the fact that it was a low one-level design suited for this stage in his career.

MOVING FROM LARGE TO SMALL SPACE

While he was married for 23 years, Tom lived in a 3,000-sq.-ft. home not far from his new home. After selling that house, he knew he wanted to live a simpler life in a home that was less expensive to operate and one that would allow him to age in place. After years as an "active consumer," Tom's large house and barn had become his own "personal museum of too much, mostly duplicate, and not very valuable stuff." When his house sold quickly, he realized he had to dispose of things in a hurry.

With his new house under construction, Tom proceeded to make piles of possessions by category: furnishings, clothing, sporting equipment, books, photographs, and so on. The first elimination was easy, but there was still plenty left that he initially considered essential. He got rid of many of his business suits and ties, and any other clothing that he hadn't worn in the last year. Once he got going, he says, "It felt like a cleansing experience in preparation for a new life that required less baggage."

Tom made regular trips to Goodwill, secondhand stores, and the local recycling center. However, after all of this purging, there was still a good deal he could not part with, so he decided to temporarily store the rest in his brother John's basement. This way, he would have time to stage his final edit and still meet his closing date.

Moving all of his material possessions was a major task and in the end, most of those things did not make the cut to his new, more fulfilling but

The owner oriented the house to the view of the wetlands, with a row of windows on this back side but no windows on the front, road-facing side (for privacy). The siding is Canadian tongue-and-groove cedar, and all landscaping is natural, with native grasses and wildflowers.

INDUCTION STOVES/COOKTOPS

Induction cooktops contain copper coils beneath the cooking surface that receive an electric current, producing a magnetic field that induces current through ferrous (magnetic) pots. This latter current heats the pots. The cooktop, however, remains relatively cool.

These cooktops are more energy efficient, heat faster, and are more consistent than traditional electric ranges and are as instantaneous as gas burners. With induction cooking, energy is supplied directly to the cooking vessel by the magnetic field, and almost all of the source energy is transferred to that vessel. With gas and traditional electric stoves, a good deal of the energy dissipates into the air and surrounding surfaces.

Induction cooktops are easy to clean because the surface is flat and smooth and does not get hot enough to make spilled food burn and stick. The burner shuts down automatically when iron or steel cookware is removed. This also means induction cooktops are safer than conventional units because there's no risk of burning little fingers. These appliances require no gas lines; and a ductless hood eliminates the need for another opening in the exterior of the house.

One of the drawbacks to induction cooking is that the pots must be compatible with the stovetop, which means you can only use pots made of magnetic materials. Another drawback is that the glass ceramic surface can be marred by a significant impact or scratched by sliding pots. Furthermore, aluminum foil can melt onto the surface, permanently damaging the cooktop. The induction stove used in this house is by Wolf (subzero-wolf.com).

TOP: The pine-covered wall in the living room was fashioned from a 100+-year-old pine tree that had to be cut down to make room for the house. Tom had the pine milled to 12-in.-wide 18-ft. lengths, stained white, and hung with antique nails. The shed roof creates high ceilings in the living area and, with windows at two heights, brings a good deal of light into the house.

ABOVE: The vintage zinc sink unit is in contrast to the cleaner contemporary design of the house. Tom repaired the zinc and added a modern faucet and fittings.

reduced existence. He says the lesson to be learned from his purge is to edit more quickly with less emotional attachment to items in your home. Tom was very selective about the furnishings he would take to his new house. Most of the large pieces were neither the size nor the aesthetic he thought would fit. So he ended up buying new and vintage items that were more appropriate to the style he wanted to achieve in his new life.

With the refrigerator, convection oven, and mechanicals in a separate utility room (behind the door to the left), the kitchen is a spare, almost spartan space. The kitchen countertop, base, and lower cabinet doors were made on site by Bernie, the carpenter. The stools came from a local craftsman in Litchfield County. The kitchen wall shelf was hand-cut from a 300-year-old piece of chestnut from a salvaged 18th-century colonial home nearby.

BUILDING FOR NEED NOT WANT

In today's society, a lot of people feel that more is more. However, when building a house, more means more construction expense, more to clean, more to maintain, and more money spent on energy. And in many cases, people don't need all of the space that they opt to build. Many homeowners report that living with less is liberating, as Tom has expressed with his new home. He owns 6 wooded acres and could have built a much larger house but decided to build just what he needed, minimizing his construction and upkeep costs. He chose not to build a garage because he felt it wasn't necessary (but he did install a plug on the outside of his house so he could power an electric car).

With energy efficiency paramount in mind, Tom paid particular attention to air-sealing the house and using mineral wool insulation combined with some spray foam in the corners. A frost-free insulated cement slab and high-efficiency windows were essential ingredients to keep his house airtight and efficient. Mini-split units were used for heating and cooling, and an energy recovery ventilator was added to ensure good interior air quality.

The "less-is-more" look extends to the design of the house, and Hicks used his architectural expertise to create interior and exterior proportions that make something special out of a simple rectangular structure. It's a fascinating mix of living space and storage in a pared-down, downsized design.

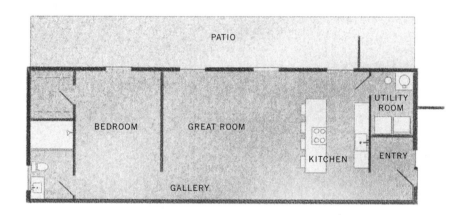

DOWNSIZING FEATURES
- One-floor living
- High ceilings
- Barrier-free shower

GREEN FEATURES
- Induction stove
- Reclaimed, local materials
- Triple-glazed windows
- Concrete floors
- Energy recovery ventilator (ERV)
- LED lights, inside and out
- Metal roof
- Natural landscaping
- Large overhangs

TOP LEFT: The rimless shower is easily accessible and appropriate for aging in place. Tiles are white subway tile, giving the room a modern and stark appearance. A heated towel rack doubles as a grab bar.

ABOVE: Storage in the living room is artfully minimal.

TOP RIGHT: The metal bed pieces were "bead blasted" (a process used to remove surface deposits by applying fine glass beads at a high pressure without damaging the surface) and then lacquer-sealed to give them a natural gray color. The shelf over the bed is from the 300-year-old wood, held up by large metal barn saddle hooks.

SKIDMORE PASSIVHAUS

CONSTRUCTION TYPE:
Site Built

ARCHITECT/GENERAL CONTRACTOR:
Jeff Stern, In Situ Architecture

PHOTOGRAPHER:
Jeremy Bittermann

LOCATION:
Portland, Ore.

SIZE:
1,965 sq. ft.

CERTIFICATIONS:
Passive House Certified (PHIUS+)

Northwest Energy Star

Earth Advantage Platinum

FOR SEVEN YEARS ARCHITECT JEFF STERN AND HIS wife, Karen Thurman, lived in a 1950s house in southwest Portland. The house was 2,800 sq. ft. with a two-car garage, which they'd purchased primarily because they were attracted to its open, airy, and modern feel. They knew the house was oversize for what they needed, and several of its rooms were rarely used. They liked the idea of building a house that was better suited to their needs, both in terms of quantity of space and quality of construction.

In addition, the house needed to accommodate separate work spaces for husband and wife. Jeff, founder of In Situ Architecture, has an office near downtown Portland but also frequently works from his home office, which doubles as a guest room. Karen does bookkeeping part time but works as a fiber artist in her studio; both spaces are in the work wing of the house.

The couple initially lived in the 1940s, 800-sq.-ft. house that was on the property they bought. They considered remodeling the house or reusing parts of it, but in the end they decided it made better sense to start over. Jeff and Karen moved to a rental for a year while they built their new house. Having to move twice allowed them to more gradually pare down their belongings and get comfortable with the idea of living in a smaller home.

BUILDING A PASSIVE HOUSE

They chose to build the house to Passive House (PH) standards because they wanted the most comfortable and energy-efficient house possible, and PH standards appealed to them as the best way to achieve that. According to Jeff and Karen, the house is "amazingly comfortable," particularly in comparison to their old leaky, poorly insulated 1950s house. The inside temperature remains comfortable for most of the year, without any heating or cooling (there is no mechanical cooling). In addition, the use of a heat recovery ventilator (HRV) means that the air is always fresh, and the house is very quiet due to the extra insulation and the minimal HVAC equipment. Jeff says that he would never build any other way.

To achieve the standards required for PH certification, the house was built to be very airtight (it tested at 0.32 ach 50, exceeding PH requirements). Triple-glazed windows and doors are extremely efficient, and various forms of insulation also help keep the house airtight and energy efficient. Rigid EPS (expanded polystyrene) was used under the slab and the footings and on the outside of the foundation, while blown-in fiberglass was used in the wall and roof cavities. The entire house was also covered in a "blanket" of rigid insulation on the exterior walls and roof.

Architect Jeff Stern was sensitive to the scale of the traditional houses in the neighborhood when designing his home. He kept the front of the house very private with few windows, while the rear space is open and expansive.

TOP LEFT: The red entrance door adds color to the monotone wood façade on the exterior. The siding is western red cedar with a semi-transparent stain.

TOP RIGHT: The space between the two areas of the house, living and work, has a pop of color with red pocket doors. Owners call it the breezeway even though it is a conditioned space.

ABOVE: The bright green AC fir plywood countertop provides a splash of color in contrast to the unpainted AC fir plywood cabinets and white walls. Multicolor chairs and a colorful clock on the wall add additional color accents to the room.

A custom steel staircase, which leads up to the loft-like second floor of the house, separates the double-height living room area from the dining room and kitchen.

The shared bathroom in the work area of the house has a trough sink and a rimless walk-in shower. At the entry, the bright red bathroom door contrasts with the white cement plaster walls beyond.

A small solar array (3.42kW) on the roof of the house produces over three-quarters of their annual electricity needs. Jeff and Karen opted to stay connected to the grid and net meter so they can get credit back in kWH when they produce more energy than they need and still get energy when there is limited sun. On the upper roof, a green living roof with a mixture of sedums (succulent plants) keeps the roof cooler, which in turn helps the PV panels work a bit more efficiently.

The house was built using an old-time method of construction called balloon framing, which helps create a more energy-efficient thermal envelope and air barrier. For this type of construction, the framing lumber is extra long and spans the two floors of the house, rather than having the floor system sitting on top of each wall. Jeff chose this method for the two-story portion of the house to minimize the amount of framing lumber required and to maximize the space for insulation.

FIRST FLOOR

SECOND FLOOR

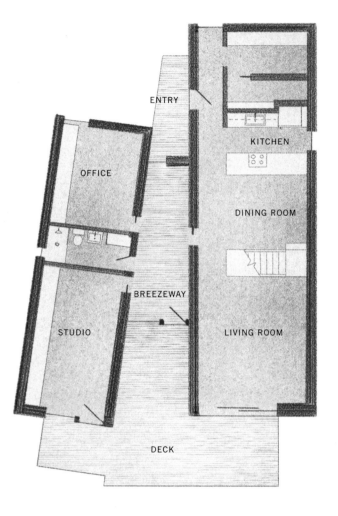

ENTRY

KITCHEN

OFFICE

DINING ROOM

BREEZEWAY

STUDIO

LIVING ROOM

DECK

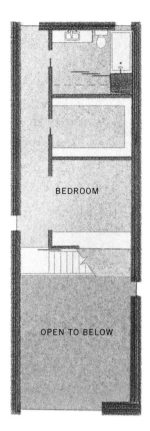

BEDROOM

OPEN TO BELOW

DOWNSIZING FEATURES
- High ceilings
- Barrier-free shower
- One-step entrance

GREEN FEATURES
- Triple-glazed windows
- South-facing windows
- Airtight construction
- Heat recovery ventilator (HRV)
- Motorized exterior aluminum shades
- Green living roof
- Photovoltaic (PV) array
- Superinsulation

MAKING A SMALL HOUSE FEEL LARGE

Jeff used several techniques to make the house feel larger than its small footprint. He created a strong connection to the site and backyard by using large windows and doors. He also created a small transition space between the two-story living wing of the house and the one-story work wing, with a fully enclosed interior "breezeway." The two-story ceiling in the living room creates a more spacious feel and allows in more light. In addition, with the bedroom open to the living room, light and the exterior views are shared with the space below; sliding doors can be closed for privacy.

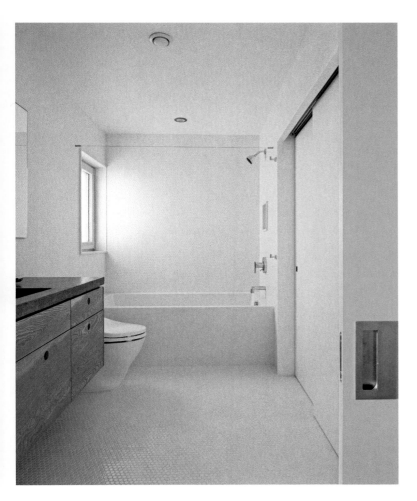

In the master bedroom on the second floor, the yellow pocket door is the accent to the stark white surfaces. Jeff built the concrete countertop himself.

PASSIVE HOUSE (PH)

The Passive House (PH), or Passivhaus, standard was first established in Germany but is now being used in many countries around the world, including the United States. (The U.S. has its own arm of the organization know as PHIUS.) It focuses on reducing energy consumption for space heating and cooling by about 90% as well as on comfort and affordability. The Passive House Planning Package (PHPP) software can be used to predict energy usage and losses for individual homes or other structures. The requirements are stringent and include maximum heating and cooling demand, total primary energy consumption, and a maximum leakage of air volume per hour at 50 pascals of pressure, which is measured with a blower door test.

Passive houses are designed with superinsulation, high-performance windows, adequate shading (for warmer months), an airtight building shell or "envelope," and the use of an energy recovery ventilator (ERV) to exchange the interior air with fresh outside air. Creating energy is not the main focus of PH structures, although some houses do include active solar systems. Passive houses are designed to save approximately 75% of the entire energy used in a house compared to average built houses. For further information about the Passive House Institute US, visit phius.org; internationally, visit passiv.de.

The one bedroom that is located on the upper floor is open to the hallway and stairs to the lower level. A bright green door opens to the closet and a yellow door to the master bathroom. The green bedside table echoes the countertop material in the kitchen.

AC FIR PLYWOOD

Plywood is an engineered lumber composed of three or more layers, which are oriented 90 degrees to one another to increase the structural stability in all directions. The letters A, B, C, and D are used to grade the visual characteristics of the veneers. These letters describe the quality of the face of the plywood, with A being the highest quality. The first letter describes the exposed visible portion of the plywood and the second letter the interior veneer. Middle layers are not graded. AC grade is the most common type of plywood.

ABOVE RIGHT AND FACING PAGE: The two "boxes" that form the wings of the house, with work spaces on the left and living on the right, each open onto the deck. South-facing motorized exterior aluminum blinds can be lowered to block unwanted solar gain in the summer.

LONGLEAF HOUSE

CONSTRUCTION TYPE:
Site Built, with Timber-Frame Elements

ARCHITECT:
Esposito Design

PHOTOGRAPHER:
Joel Esposito

LOCATION:
Saint Johns, Fla.

SIZE:
1,790 sq. ft.

HERS INDEX:
58 (see the sidebar on p. 149)

WHEN BOB AND MONICA ESPOSITO BECAME EMPTY nesters, they had some fairly standard requirements: They wanted a home that was more energy efficient than their previous 2,500-sq.-ft. house; a home with lower operating costs; and one that was suitable for aging-in-place, as well as for family gatherings and entertaining.

The location they chose is on the historic Lake Beluthahatchee in northeast Florida, sited across the lake from the house of the late author and activist Stetson Kennedy. The house was designed to take advantage of the surrounding natural environment with views of the beautiful lake, incorporating features that harmonize with its surroundings, such as expansive open-frame porches.

A DESIGNER'S HOME

Bob, a Certified Professional Building Designer, designed the house along with his son Joel. Father and son work together professionally as Esposito Design, a boutique custom home design studio, focusing on practical and attractive architecture, built to meet their clients' lifestyle.

The primary design strategy for this house was to display an old Florida aesthetic while employing some of the latest and most efficient sustainable building products. The house was also designed so the couple could age in place. Quality was the priority over quantity. Minimal hallways (see the sidebar on p. 63) add to the thoughtful use of a small footprint.

AGING IN PLACE

All primary living spaces, the master suite, and the laundry room are located on the first floor. Upstairs, the back bedroom facing the lake is used for visiting family and guests, while the front room is used as a home office/studio. The staircase to the second floor is designed to accommodate a potential chair lift should one ever be needed. A barrier-free shower was installed in the master bathroom for safety and any unforeseen eventualities.

When Monica and Bob began to dispose of their possessions, like many of the other homeowners in this book who downsized, they were surprised at how much stuff they had acquired over the years—things they no longer needed. To sort through it all, they separated everything into three categories: must keep, offer to family and friends, and donate to charitable organizations. Most of the furniture from their old house was given to family and friends; only furniture for the guest room was moved

The shape and appearance of the house were inspired by traditional southern architectural styles: simple/utilitarian forms, gable roofs, shed dormers, and timber-frame porches. Fiber cement siding and a standing-seam metal roof are long-lasting materials that make the house mostly maintenance free.

Flooring in the kitchen and throughout most of the house is engineered hardwood, the dark wood offering a stark contrast to the predominantly white kitchen. Cabinetry is efficiently designed with lots of storage space, and the refrigerator and microwave are mini undercounter appliances.

to the new house. For Monica, purging so many things was truly a liberating experience.

As part of their plan for retirement, the couple identified the annual cost of operating a home as a way to reduce expenses. Their previous home was built 20 years ago to meet basic building code requirements with prevailing methods and materials of the day. It was not an energy-efficient system and would have been cost-prohibitive to modify. The lack of modern efficiencies coupled with too many rooms and unnecessary square footage led to their decision to build this new home.

Although the house is smaller in terms of square footage, it actually feels bigger than the house they lived in before. Monica and Bob attribute this to the higher ceilings, large windows, front and rear porches, and more efficient use of space. It feels like an upgrade, even though it's technically smaller. They say it is analogous to wearing tailored/fitted clothing—less room but you feel better wearing it. There's no doubt that the move has impacted the couple's daily routines, habits, and moods in a very positive way.

The claw-foot tub sits in a comfortable niche in the master bathroom. The shower is barrier-free for safety and to support aging in place.

The barn door to the pantry adds rustic charm to the house and takes up less space than a swinging door.

THE CASE FOR MINIMAL HALLWAYS

One way to reduce square footage in a floor plan is to minimize the hallways throughout the house. Halls that are just pathways cost money per square foot to build, maintain, and heat/cool. By having a more open floor plan, the need for hallways is mostly eliminated. Making the circulation area between rooms functional, such as adding a sitting or work area between spaces, eliminates the waste of narrow hallways that are nonfunctional. In the Longleaf House there are almost no hallways at all, except for a short hall between the kitchen and master bedroom. When building a small house, the usable space should be maximized and any wasted footage eliminated.

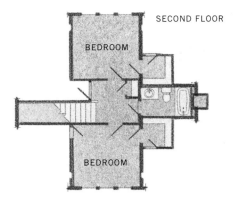

SECOND FLOOR

BEDROOM

BEDROOM

Custom beams add to the charm of the southern design, while ceiling fans are strategically placed throughout the house for additional air circulation during the warm months.

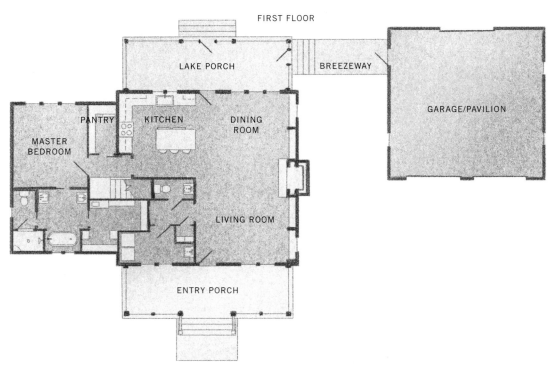

FIRST FLOOR

LAKE PORCH

BREEZEWAY

GARAGE/PAVILION

PANTRY

KITCHEN

DINING ROOM

MASTER BEDROOM

LIVING ROOM

ENTRY PORCH

DOWNSIZING FEATURES

- Undercounter appliances
- Minimal hallways
- Barrier-free shower
- Large windows
- Multipurpose rooms
- Master bedroom on first floor
- Large porches to expand living space

GREEN FEATURES

- Super sealing
- Open-cell spray insulation
- Metal roofing
- High-performance windows
- Induction range
- LED lights
- Native plantings
- ENERGY STAR appliances

RIGHT: The rear of the house has an expansive screened porch for outdoor living and family entertaining. The rear dormer mirrors the dormer on the front side.

BELOW: The garage was designed with roll-up doors on both sides to create an outdoor pavilion for large family gatherings.

The front entrance has the charm of a typical southern lake cottage with the timber-frame overhang and front door with glazing. The multiple tall windows add to the appeal of the entryway.

PINWHEEL ADU

CONSTRUCTION TYPE:
Site Built

ARCHITECT:
Scott Mooney, SRG
Partnership

PHOTOGRAPHER:
Olivia Ashton

LOCATION:
Portland, Ore.

SIZE:
624 sq. ft.

ARCHITECT SCOTT MOONEY WAS LOOKING FOR A house to purchase in the Richmond neighborhood of southeast Portland, but wanted one with a lot that could accommodate an accessory dwelling unit (ADU) (see the sidebar on p. 71). He found what he was looking for in a 1950s bungalow that was 840 sq. ft. on a 5,000-sq.-ft. lot. With the existing house's relatively small footprint and position toward the front half of the property, it was an ideal location to eventually build a smaller home in the rear. Scott lived in the bungalow for eight years and when he got together with Lauren Shumaker, a construction engineer, together they planned to build the ADU on the property behind the house. When the ADU was finally complete they rented out the original bungalow and moved into the ADU.

MOTIVATED TO BUILD SMALL

The couple wanted to provide a built example of how good design can simultaneously serve to be beautiful, enhance the quality of life, and reduce the size of our physical and ecological footprint. Scott's volunteer work designing Pods to help address the homeless crisis in his community helped prepare him to build his own small ADU. In his professional career with civic and higher-education projects, he also tried to utilize space most efficiently, finding ways to do more with less. Building the 624-sq.-ft. ADU was the product of much of his earlier learning.

Since Scott and Lauren were both at their jobs all week, they were able to work on the house only on weekends and evenings. It took eight months to complete their project. While the lion's share of the work was done by their contractor partners at TaylorSmith Sustainable Construction, the couple helped with some of the finish work, including installing the cabinet faces and hardware. Aside from the pavers, they also did all of the exterior landscape work themselves, including moving 10 yd. of soil and 2 tons of rock for their garden and backyard.

STORAGE AREAS CREATE A PINWHEEL

The house was designed so that all of the homeowners' everyday belongings could be stored in four storage blocks. They house bicycles, tools, and other utilitarian objects such as the electric hot-water heater. These storage blocks are organized in a pinwheel fashion that opens up at the corners, with large expanses of glass stitching the blocks together as you move around the house. In addition to storage, these recesses provide solar shading to the south, a covered porch to the north, and areas where

(Continued on p. 70)

The ADU sits on a 5,000-sq.-ft. property that also houses the original house and a place to park two cars and a motorcycle. The building is clad in sustainably harvested western red cedar, and the roof is dark gray standing-seam metal. With the easy connection through the slider to the outdoor patio, the house feels more expansive than it is and forms a strong connection to the outdoors.

ABOVE: All of the interior cabinetry was made at ADX, a local fabrication facility, and the appliances are electric "apartment size." The center island provides an excellent workspace as well as a comfortable dining area for the couple and their friends.

RIGHT: The kitchen and living room occupy the full width of the house in a floor plan that is compact, efficiently organized, and beautifully simple. The space above the bedrooms (at left) is a shallow loft that can accommodate overnight guests.

ABOVE: Shelving in the living room holds Scotts' considerable collection of record albums. Flooring throughout the house is sealed concrete. The living room opens onto a patio through the wall-to-wall slider at the end of the room, providing another comfortable eating area during the warmer months.

LEFT: The master bedroom has plenty of cabinetry for storage and a large window to bring in natural daylighting. The small opening below the window is their Freedom Pet Pass doggie wall (which passes California's Title 24 energy-efficiency requirements).

the blocks can run between the inside and the outside of the house, seamlessly blending the interior and exterior environments.

INCORPORATING SUSTAINABILITY

The couple wanted to build the house with the most efficient and sustainable methods. They used low-flow fixtures; a highly insulated wall assembly; high-performing windows; ample daylighting; passive cooling; responsible, nontoxic materials (such as FSC framing and siding); and an efficient ductless mini-split for heating and cooling. They tracked energy use over the first year of operation and later installed a right-size photovoltaic array (not installed until after the photos were taken) to offset the energy use of both the ADU and the existing home. This allows the entire property to operate without the use of fossil fuels. By leaving the flooring as raw concrete and building all of the cabinetry out of plywood, the couple sought

a more sustainable and healthier interior environment, minimizing the amount of adhesives and finishes that would need to be introduced into the space.

LIVING IN THE ADU

It took Scott and Lauren many rounds of purging in order to get rid of enough of their things to move into the new house, but they say it was a liberating process. They made sure that each object they retained was something that was either meaningful or useful to them on a day-to-day basis. "While a handful of objects that had some sentimental value did not make the cut," they say, "donating the vast majority to thrift stores gave us some satisfaction that they would find a second life out in the world."

DOWNSIZING FEATURES
• Vaulted ceiling
• Whole wall opening to the exterior
• Abundance of storage spaces
• Pocket doors

GREEN FEATURES
• High R-sheathing
• High-performance glazing
• Recycled metal roofing
• Forest Stewardship Council (FSC)-certified wood
• Low-flow faucets
• Superinsulation
• Daylighting
• Passive cooling
• Nontoxic materials
• Local materials
• Ductless mini-split
• Photovoltaic (PV) array

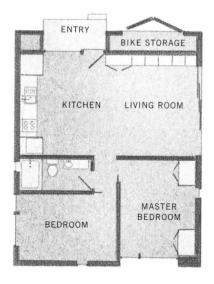

The only sacrifice the couple has made in living in the ADU is being farther back from the street and feeling less connected with the daily activity going on in the neighborhood. However, they say the large windows in the house give them more opportunity to connect with nature.

Because of both their professional experience and building skills, Lauren and Scott were able to keep the labor costs down. They were also careful about the materials they used; they needed to be sustainable, efficient, and functionable. "We love our smaller space," Scott says. "It has forced us to simplify in the best ways possible and hold on to only things that we value the most in our lives."

ACCESSORY DWELLING UNITS (ADUS)

ADUs are a second small dwelling on the same grounds as (or attached to) a regular single-family house, such as an apartment over a garage, a small house on a foundation in the backyard, a basement apartment, a granny flat, an in-law apartment, or a house in place of a garage (known in Canada as a laneway house).

Legally, an ADU is part of the same property as the main home and cannot be bought or sold separately; the owner of the main house owns the ADU. Often, family members, elderly parents, or young adult children occupy these houses. Sometimes parents will move into the ADU when they are empty nesters and give the main house to their adult children with growing families. Some people build ADUs as an extra source of income, in those areas where that is allowed.

There are various restrictions for ADUs depending on the location: how big they can be, who can live there, how many residents there can be, as well as the configuration and materials used. In the city of Portland, the size of the house could only be 75% of the usable square footage of the existing house, up to 800 sq. ft. The original house on this property was a 1950s 840-sq.-ft. bungalow, limiting the interior space of the ADU to a maximum of 630 sq. ft. (The ADU is 624 sq. ft.) Unlike tiny houses, they must meet the same regulations and codes as the primary residence. (Tiny houses are considered mobile and do not meet state and city codes.)

MAINE CAMP REBOOT

CONSTRUCTION TYPE:
Site Built

ARCHITECT/BUILDER:
GO Logic

PROJECT ARCHITECT:
Gunther Kragler,
GO Logic

PHOTOGRAPHER:
Josh Gerritsen Media
(unless otherwise noted)

LOCATION:
Palermo, Maine

SIZE:
1,100 sq. ft.

OWNERS BETSY AND JON WANTED TO DOWNSIZE once their four children were grown and out of the house. Both had recently retired: Jon from teaching, and Betsy from speech pathology. They put their larger house in China, Maine, on the market toward the end of the construction process for this new house, and, luckily for them, the house sold right away.

THE DOWNSIZING PROCESS

The process of downsizing, in this case moving from a 2,600-sq.-ft. house to a 1,100-sq.-ft. one, involved purging all of the furniture and other possessions that would not fit into this smaller space. Betsy and Jon had to dispose of 30 years of stuff, and they still work hard at not accumulating more. Now, if something new comes into the house, something else must be thrown out.

Their previous home was on a main road with lots of traffic, so they were able to hold several yard sales, which benefited a Maine-based children's cancer program their daughter had been a part of. They also gave large or specialty items to the local Habitat for Humanity ReStore and a church-based program that was willing to pick up larger pieces of furniture. Some furniture items were sold with the house and others went to a local antique dealer. Only the essentials and very special pieces were kept, such as their original mid-century modern dining table set (seen in the top photo on p. 75).

The essential requirements in designing the house, along with a predetermined budget, were a single-level space and a compact footprint so that the house could be Betsy and Jon's forever home. Initially, they were concerned that 1,100 sq. ft. would be too small, but architect Gunther Kragler assured them that with 9$\frac{1}{2}$-ft. ceilings and all of the glass that would be in the house it would feel surprisingly spacious. Betsy says his prediction was true—she says it feels really comfortable and living there is just "like being on vacation."

KEEPING IT EARTH-FRIENDLY

Betsy and Jon wanted a downsized house, but one that was highly energy efficient and that would sit gently on the earth. Local architectural firm GO Logic has a great reputation for ecofriendly construction so it was a logical choice to design the house. Betsy and Jon chose a remote site half a mile off the main road, where connecting to the power grid would have been uneconomical; as a result, the house was built 100% off the grid.

The low-pitched standing-seam metal roof spans a two-car garage at its north side and 1,100 sq. ft. of conditioned living space at its south. The structure has 24 photovoltaic (PV) panels that generate 6.7 kW, enough to satisfy everyday electrical needs. Sixteen deep-cycle batteries store surplus electricity, while a small propane generator provides backup and emergency power.

With a large window over the sink, the compact kitchen feels open and spacious. The cabinetry with laminate countertops is from IKEA, while the open, adjustable shelving system by Rakks provides flexibility and functionality.

Aside from the remote, rural location, the biggest challenge for the architect was designing the house to the site in an affordable manner. The house occupies a narrow shelf of land along the shore of a secluded pond in central Maine with beautiful water views to the west. However, its orientation was less than optimal for solar power and the topography was somewhat problematic. With ledge outcroppings to the east and a deep incline

down to the pond on the west, the house had to be skillfully sited between these two obstacles, which determined the width of the house.

Another challenge was creating enough roof area to install a large solar array on the house, which was required to cover all of the electrical loads for this off-the-grid structure. Challenges also presented themselves when balancing the needs of solar orientation (to the south) to heat and power

RIGHT: The dining room is a simple, flexible open space that shares a large window with the living area that looks out onto the pond. The owners mid-century dining set, with table and chairs that survived the purge, is the focus of the space. The dark wood of the dining set is complemented by lighter wood tones in the kitchen and living room.

BELOW: The twin bedrooms at the far end of the house are both small, but each has large windows that bring in lots of light and views to the natural surroundings. The smaller windows face south, critical for solar gain; the floor-to-ceiling windows face the fire pit and pond.

the home, with the predominant view of the property and pond (to the west).

GO Logic was able to balance the views of the property and performance to heat the home as well as embrace the property's natural surroundings. To collect enough energy to run the house, architect Gunther Kragler gave the building a simple, boxlike form topped with a finlike array of photovoltaic panels. Mounted in orderly ranks across the building's long axis, the panels became as integral to the house's aesthetic as they are to its function. By

maximizing the view, GO Logic flawlessly integrated interior and exterior spaces.

LIVING OFF-THE-GRID

Although the owners choose not to certify the house, it was built to Passive House standards. It is totally off-the-grid, with all electrical requirements provided by the photovoltaic panel array that spans the roof of the house.

Superinsulated with mineral wool, the house's air-sealed Passive House building shell and triple-

glazed windows and doors, along with passive solar gain from the bedrooms' south-facing glass, reduce the demand for supplemental heat to a level that can be handled by one small propane heater. Thermal mass from the polished concrete floors helps to release heat in the colder months and keep the house cool in the warmer months.

SMALL SPACE, LARGE IMPRESSION

The house's primary interior spaces, a great room and two mirror-image bedroom suites, are com-

pact, but large windows and glass doors open every room to the outdoors, enhancing the sense of space. The screened porch adds flexibility, serving as an open-air living room during the warmer months. Removable storm panels keep it comfortable well into the colder months. Closets were located in unheated areas, and a large, easily accessible attic minimizes the volume of interior space devoted to storage. High ceilings and large windows give the house a more expansive feeling than the small footprint actually provides.

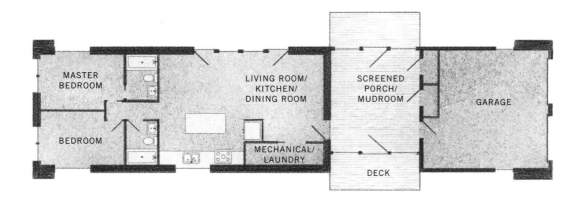

DOWNSIZING FEATURES
- One-floor living
- Flexible spaces
- High ceilings
- Expansive windows
- Easy access to exterior spaces
- Barrier-free shower
- Wall reinforced for future grab bars

GREEN FEATURES
- Photovoltaic (PV) panels
- Standing-seam metal roof
- Storage batteries

- Propane generator
- Triple-glazed windows and doors
- Built to Passive House standard
- 100% off-grid
- Locally harvested wood
- Recycled metal roof
- Mineral wool insulation
- No air conditioning
- Energy recovery ventilator (ERV)
- Propane back-up generator
- Natural landscaping
- LED lights
- Thermal mass

MINERAL WOOL INSULATION

Mineral wool (which is also known as rock wool) is made from melted stone or silica and recycled industrial slag from steel mills. It is then spun with a stream of air or steam into a fiber at high temperatures, much like the process of making cotton candy. Mineral wool insulation is available in many forms, as slabs or batts for walls, loose fibers to be blown in, and other specific forms. It is a desirable insulation because of its acoustic, thermal, and fire-resistant properties in addition to its resis-tance to rot, mold, fungi, insects, and vermin. The batts will not take on water but will allow trapped moisture to pass through and escape. With its high R-value (approximately 3.7 to 4.2 per inch) and contents from recycled materials and itself recycla-ble, it is considered a very green product. Mineral wool insulation was used on the exterior side of the wall system in this house. For further information check the website: mima.info.

SCREENED PORCHES

Screened porches can provide a good amount of extra living and entertaining space, which is a significant bonus for a small house. As shown below, the porch in this house connects the living spaces (left) and garage (right), offering a view through the building to the pond. It also serves as the house's main entrance. The screened porch doubles as an outdoor living room during the warmer months. In the colder months, the owners insert glass storm windows to weatherize the porch and continue to use it throughout the year. With the glass inserted, it's comfortable enough that they can even put their Christmas tree in this space.

THE BEACH COTTAGE

CONSTRUCTION TYPE:
Renovation

DESIGNER/DEVELOPER:
Steve Hoiles

PHOTOGRAPHER:
Darren Bradley/OTTO
(unless otherwise noted)

LOCATION:
Encinitas, Calif.

SIZE:
1,698 sq. ft.

THERE WERE A COUPLE OF REASONS WHY DESIGNER/ developer Steve Hoiles and his wife, Elizabeth, decided to move from their 2,852-sq.-ft. house in North Vancouver, British Columbia, Canada, to Encinitas, Calif. For one, the exchange rate from Canadian to American dollars was advantageous, and the economy in the United States was showing signs of recovery. They decided to take advantage of the disparity in the worth of their dollars and move to a warmer climate with a beach and surf lifestyle. And perhaps most important, their main objective was to live simpler in a small home with lots of outdoor living space.

A NEW BEGINNING IN THE UNITED STATES

When the Hoiles found this 1957 ranch house in 2012, there was evidence of termites and dry rot and the house was generally looking tired, but these were not intolerable issues initially. The family of four lived in the house as it was for four years before they began the remodel that better reflects their design aesthetic and space needs, which included a master bedroom and bathroom, a walk-in closet, and an office/flex/extra bedroom space. The rear of the house would also be opened up to bring in more light and provide a better outside living experience.

The location couldn't have been better: just two blocks from the beach on a dead-end street with only 14 homes and a great sense of community. The area is walkable and just a bike ride away from surf, school, food, and other amenities.

UPGRADING BUT NOT EXPANDING

In addition to bringing the single-level house up to his and his wife's design aesthetic, Steve needed to upgrade the house to meet current codes and replace the termite- and mold-infested areas. During the four years the family lived in the house before the renovation, Steve was perpetually in design development mode. In his original scheme, he was going to add on 500 sq. ft. to the existing 1,698-sq.-ft. footprint. However, after slow deliberation, many floor plan iterations, and endless discussions with Elizabeth, an industrial designer, they concluded that the extra 500 sq. ft. really wouldn't improve the quality of their or their children's future life.

Instead, they crafted a floor plan that was highly functional for their family's needs. Steve updated front and back outdoor living spaces, increased storage capacity as creatively as possible, and added a second bathroom. He removed two segregated rooms to introduce a new flex room that acts as Steve's office or as a guest room when extended family and friends visit from Canada.

Although the original form of the house was maintained, the exterior was updated in the renovation with a new standing-seam metal roof, new custom garage door, new windows and door, and extensive landscaping. The permeable hexagonal pavers were there in the original house.

Bottom photo courtesy of Surfside Projects

ENVIRONMENTALLY FRIENDLY CHOICES

Steve essentially kept the footprint of the house the same size and reused as many materials as possible. To create the new garage door, he bought a standard metal door and glued/nailed redwood boards recycled from an existing interior wall inside the house.

With much of California still suffering from drought, Steve tried to minimize water use on the property. He replaced the front lawn with Palm Springs Gold, a product composed of crushed decomposed granite, crushed stone, mica, and gravel. As part of Steve's xeriscaping plan, he planted drought-tolerant plants. In the interior of the house, he used all low-flow faucets and shower-heads and dual-flush toilets.

Steve has focused on designing modernist, sustainable small houses since he began his development company in 2004. Concise and efficient use of space with access to outdoor spaces is integral to his design theories. He says the ultimate feature in designing a smaller house is having an open floor plan, which he created magnificently in this "new old" house. According to Steve, remodeling this house was the best housing decision the family ever made, allowing them to enjoy a "big lifestyle in a small shelter."

Owner Steve Hoiles took the photo that adorns the wall in the living room at the local beach just two blocks away from his home. The photo was printed on an 8-ft. by 14-ft. adhesive vinyl and applied to the finished wall like a sticker. The vaulted ceiling and skylights add to the bright and airy interior.

ABOVE LEFT: The kitchen was designed to provide maximum storage and countertop space. High-quality marine-grade plywood was used with a Douglas fir veneer as the finished doors of the cabinets, inspired by Scandinavian design. The countertops are engineered quartz.

ABOVE RIGHT: The flooring throughout the house is engineered hardwood made of brushed natural white oak. The clerestory windows add to the natural daylighting coming into the house. The unusual light fixture over the dining table, created by the designer's wife Elizabeth, was made by weaving four black cord lights together.

LEFT: The master bedroom opens onto the exterior deck, which is built from white ash that has been thermally modified, creating a very durable, water-resistant product. As part of the xeriscaping plan, Palm Springs Gold gravel was used in the planting beds, which include drought-tolerant plants that can tolerate coastal conditions.

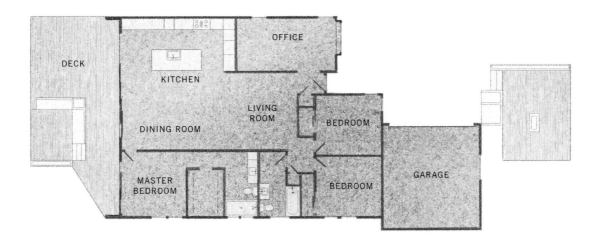

ENGINEERED QUARTZ COUNTERTOPS

Quartz countertops are becoming increasingly popular because of their durability and the rich variety of colors available. Engineered quartz is a composite material made of crushed stone bound together with some type of adhesive such as resin.

Quartz is nonporous, making it relatively bacteria-free, scratch resistant, and less likely to stain than some other stone slabs. Because it is manufactured, there is less veining and pattern in the stone, which may be a positive or a negative depending on personal preference. On the negative side, quartz can be damaged by excessive heat. It is also more expensive than some other popular stones, such as granite. To check out the quartz countertops used in this house, go to pentalquartz.com

DOWNSIZING FEATURES
- One-floor living
- Large outdoor space
- Vaulted ceiling
- Daylighting
- Open-concept plan

GREEN FEATURES
- Remodeled existing house
- Recycled materials
- Permeable paving
- Natural ventilation
- LED lights
- Engineered wood
- Blown-in cellulose insulation
- Drought-tolerant plants
- Dual-flush toilets
- Low-flow faucets and showerheads
- Induction cooktop
- Large overhangs
- Quartz countertops

The back of the house was opened up with sliding glass doors and an expansive deck that graciously provides for indoor/outdoor living.

Photo at right courtesy of Surfside Projects

PERMEABLE PAVING

With permeable paving, water flows through the ground naturally, filtering out surface pollutants and helping water to remain clean. By contrast, asphalt and concrete don't allow water to seep into the ground, but rather force it into manmade channels, collecting surface pollutants along the way. A variety of pervious paving materials are available, including porous grass pavers, crushed oyster shells, gravel, crushed stone, and the permeable pavers used at The Beach Cottage. Though these materials generally cost as much as 40% more than asphalt surfaces, many are maintenance free and better for the environment.

HERON ROCK
COTTAGE

CONSTRUCTION TYPE:
Kit House/Post and Beam

MANUFACTURER:
Lindal Cedar Homes

PHOTOGRAPHER:
Patrick Barta

LOCATION:
Whidbey Island,
Wash.

SIZE:
1,812 sq. ft.

SOME PEOPLE DOWNSIZE TO REDUCE THEIR MAIN-tenance and upkeep expenses, while others become empty nesters and need less space. Another reason why couples choose to live smaller is because they get married and need to combine two households into one. That was the case with Nancy and Ron.

Nancy had owned the property on which this downsized house now stands on Whidbey Island for 32 years. Initially, the land had just a rough "sleep" house on it that eventually morphed into a summer cottage. When she got divorced, she was the sole owner of the property and decided to develop the land and remodel the house as a year-round space. She brought in power and telephone service, drilled a well, and had a septic system installed. At the same time, she established a second building site closer to the bluff with the dream of one day building her dream home on that site, with the cottage becoming a guesthouse.

Thirteen years ago, just as Nancy was completing the development of the land, she and Ron got together. She was working full time and living in an apartment in Seattle; Ron was semi-retired. Nancy put many of her belongings in storage and moved into Ron's 1,800-sq.-ft. house in Seattle. Together they traveled between Ron's house and the small cottage in Whidbey Island. Before Nancy retired she added 600 sq. ft. onto the cottage to make it more livable, resulting in a 996-sq.-ft. space.

NANCY AND RON TOGETHER

When Nancy retired five years ago the couple decided to get married; they then had to decide where they were going to live. Ultimately, they choose to make Whidbey Island their primary residence and to build their forever home. (The small 996-sq.-ft. cottage is now an Airbnb.) Ron sold his Seattle home to finance the construction of the new house. Nancy also sold her apartment in Seattle. They consolidated their belongings into Heron Rock Cottage, which is now their main full-time residence.

At the tender age of 70, it was difficult for Ron to leave his beloved Seattle (as Nancy says, "Seattle is in his DNA"), so to make the move less of a loss for him, they bought a small 500-sq.-ft. co-op in Seattle. That meant he could still enjoy his Seattle roots, friends, and cultural attractions, and they would be close to their medical center and Nancy's mother. Having a place in Seattle also meant Ron could continue to substitute teach at the high school he had worked at for 43 years.

The house sits on a bluff above Puget Sound with floor-to-ceiling triple-glazed windows that offer unobstructed views of the waterway.

DOWNSIZING TWO HOUSES INTO ONE

Ron had the most trouble downsizing—in Nancy's words, "Each item he gave up was like minor surgery." As a beloved high-school teacher, Ron keeps in touch with many of his students on Facebook, and he put out the word that he had lots of furnishings and art to give away. He was delighted to give these items to the students, as if they were his own children.

Nancy had an easier time downsizing as she'd done it several times before. She was able to give away furnishings and other things with greater ease and keep just those items that would create a cohesive design style for their new home. She says it's a process sifting through belongings, but one that gets easier when you realize these things are not being used.

The living/dining space is the room with the view (through a wall of energy-efficient windows with argon-filled low-e glass). The post-and-beam building system is clearly visible in the laminated Douglas fir beams and clear fir trim. Radiant heat is delivered through water-filled tubes embedded in the polished concrete floor, which is scored into 5-ft.-square sections that match the spacing of the beams and windows.

THE NEW HOUSE

For their new home, Nancy and Ron favored a prefabricated approach, and they chose Lindal Homes because their post-and-beam construction allowed them to incorporate a massive wall of windows to take advantage of the water view. They also needed enough wall space to display their artwork (both Nancy and Ron are regionally recognized artists) and an art studio so they could contin-ue creating art. Other requirements were one-level living and low maintenance; the corrugated metal siding, cement board panels, and vinyl windows were all chosen with minimal maintenance in mind, and the landscaping requires little maintenance or watering.

Nancy and Ron also wanted two distinct living spaces, one zone for their personal living space with a great room and master suite and the other "away zone" to include a guest suite, office space, and art studio. The entry gallery connects the two zones and allows for privacy and acoustic separation.

BARRIER-FREE SHOWERS

Barrier-free, or curbless, showers that are designed to provide a safe and convenient shower experience are growing in popularity. A curbless shower floor is flush with the rest of the bathroom flooring and safe for people with disabilities as well as healthy adults. It eliminates the risk of tripping on a curb getting into a shower, adhering to the concept of Universal Design, which specifies that design should be accessible to all people at every stage of changing lives. As such, the controls and storage niches should be reachable by a seated person and the shower should have an adjustable handheld spray. Walls should be reinforced to support grab bars and built-in seats.

Barrier-free showers must be constructed with the slope of the floor directing the water toward the drain, keeping the water in the shower area. Some curbless showers are created with prefabricated shower trays, which are flush with the rest of the bathroom floor. Other barrier showers are custom made with a sloped mortar bed. Wet rooms are also becoming more common. These are showers with no barriers that share the bathroom space without separating walls. The flooring needs to be sloped toward the floor drain.

LEFT AND BELOW: The curbless shower in the Asian-inspired master suite transitions seam-lessly from the bathroom floor to the shower.

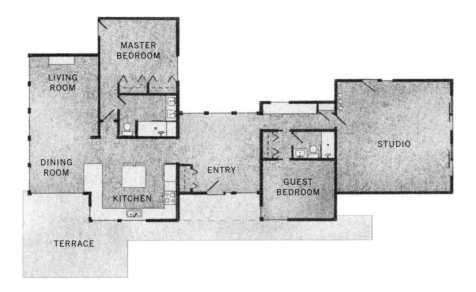

MASTER BEDROOM

LIVING ROOM

STUDIO

DINING ROOM

ENTRY

GUEST BEDROOM

KITCHEN

TERRACE

DOWNSIZING FEATURES

- High ceilings
- Barrier-free shower
- No steps (either inside or to the exterior)
- Extra bedroom en suite on other side of house for future caregiver
- Voice-activated system

GREEN FEATURES

- LED lights
- Cement floors
- Argon-filled low-e windows
- Solar-powered exterior window blinds
- Natural ventilation
- ENERGY STAR appliances
- Hydronic radiant heat
- Oxygen water purification system

AN ARTFUL HOME

This house is clearly the residence of two artists. Sculptures and pottery they created abound throughout the house. As a practical project, Ron built the fireplace surround as an assembly of cement board panels, framed by and fastened with stainless-steel screws, all surplus from the house siding.

And then there is the garden and the view. In Nancy's words, "We love the view and how it is a part of the house, along with the gardens we have put in too. It truly minimizes the distinction between inside and out—living with nature as a part of our everyday life. With the gardens lit with floodlights, both day and night the views are as much a part of the house as the paintings on the walls."

LEFT: Just beyond the entrance to the house, the comfortable kitchen is an informal gathering space. Expansive windows over the sink and clerestory windows bring in lots of light; the lower windows provide views to the Japanese garden and Puget Sound beyond.

BELOW: A hallway from the entry leads to the studio at the south end of the house, where Nancy and Ron both continue to create their art. There's plenty of room for storage of art supplies and works in progress and display of finished pieces. Operable windows and doors provide ventilation and natural light.

FACING PAGE TOP: The dining area flows through to the outdoor seating area. A woven cedar fence, crowned with wisteria, screens a nearby house and provides privacy.

FACING PAGE BOTTOM LEFT: The personal living zone and the working/guest zone are linked by an entry gallery that houses ancient Japanese art along with works by modern regional artists. The entrance to the house opens onto a beautiful Japanese-style garden.

FACING PAGE BOTTOM RIGHT: Zones of circulation in the house were designed to be functional spaces. An example is the hallway from the entrance to the artists' studio, which serves as the couple's home office space with a 12-ft.-long desk for two.

ABOVE: By turning the house 90 degrees on the property, a 25-ft. corridor was created on the west, entry side of the house that is bathed in sunshine all afternoon. The corrugated steel and cement board panel siding require little maintenance.

CARRIAGE HOUSE

CONSTRUCTION TYPE:
Renovation

ARCHITECT:
Shawn Buehler,
Bennett Frank McCarthy
Architects, Inc.

PHOTOGRAPHER:
Bennett Frank McCarthy
Architects, Inc.

LOCATION:
Washington, D.C.

SIZE:
1,650 sq. ft.

FOR SOME PEOPLE, DOWNSIZING ONCE IS CHALlenge enough. Others we might classify as "serial downsizers." Take Anna and Dan, for example: they've moved five times in Washington, D.C., over the past 25 years. Prior to moving to this unique home, they lived in a more traditional 4,000-sq.-ft. house and then moved to a renovated laundry that was about 2,300 sq. ft. Each move has been a succession of downsizes.

Anna explains that the houses they could afford were always along the edges of neighborhoods, which had suffered from neglect and blight. All their renovations were done because they fell madly in love with the properties that needed some TLC. That's what happened with the Carriage House, and they couldn't bear the idea that someone else might do something awful to it.

A HOME WITH A HISTORY

The house is located in Blagden Alley, which is in the Historic District in the Shaw neighborhood of D.C. The area has recently become home to restaurants with Michelin-starred chefs, but it was not always so fashionable: It is said that Eleanor Roosevelt once dubbed it the country's most despicable alley.

The house was originally built as a commercial alley structure over 100 years ago by Samuel Huntress, a coal oil salesman. He also built a row house on the property in front of the alley structure, but that fell into disrepair and was demolished, leaving only a vacant lot with the alley structure at the rear of it. Anna and Dan bought the property that way and converted the alley structure into their home in 2011. A few years later, this pioneering couple rebuilt the row house into a three-unit condo, maintaining the original vintage feel of the neighborhood while also making some rental money off the property.

Anna and Dan got rid of many of their things when they downsized into the carriage house. It helped that they own GoodWood, an antique/vintage store, which meant that they could simply move some of the excess items to the store. The only thing that made the move with them was their bed. In a somewhat unusual arrangement, most of the furniture currently in the house, other than the bed, comes and goes to GoodWood.

CONVERTING THE BUILDING TO A HOME

The design for the home is based on an open plan with just a few large spaces rather than several smaller ones, making the house feel bigger than it would with closed-off rooms. The entire ground floor was per-

FACING PAGE: Built by a coal oil salesman, the building served a variety of industrial purposes over its 100-year history prior to its renovation.

With no barrier walls on the first floor, air and light can flow through the building from front to back. The flooring is a concrete slab that was cleaned and sealed.

REFURBISHING HISTORICAL BUILDINGS

According to architect Shawn Buehler, it is most important to start with a detailed survey of the existing building to see what it can contribute to the finished home. He says, "The more you can keep and express, the better." In the case of the Carriage House, he saw the existing exposed brick walls, the bar joists (supports used to hold up the second floor, which can be seen from the lower floor), and the structural columns as an asset to the finished design. The steel brackets, used as lumber racks in the original building, were salvaged to become steel brackets for the kitchen shelving.

ceived as the entertaining level (kitchen/dining and lounge), which the owners use as a dinner club, hiring chefs to cook for the parties they host periodically. The second floor is the living level, with sleeping and living spaces (but no enclosed bedroom). Architect Shawn Buehler says the house was designed specifically with open spans from front to back to allow light to come in from both directions. Existing bar joists were left exposed, as were roof beams and support columns. The original building had no interior stairs so the second floor could only be accessed from the outside, which meant new interior stairs had to be added.

Mindful of budget, the owners decided to keep the existing plywood floor upstairs and paint it with a blue and gray chevron pattern rather than putting down a new floor.

A wall of built-in cabinets organizes the second-floor studio living space while providing much-needed storage.

FIRST FLOOR

SECOND FLOOR

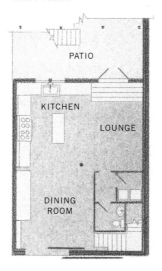

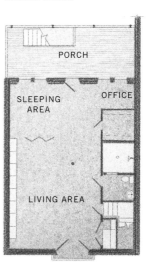

The first floor is set up to allow the owners to host dinner parties in a setting that celebrates the urban character of their Blagden Alley neighborhood. Open shelving provides plenty of storage without blocking the natural brick walls and windows. The refrigerator and freezer are both below the countertop to keep the space uncluttered.

ABOVE: All of the exterior walls were kept intact, including the first-floor brick walls, which were left exposed and unpainted to showcase the history of the structure. Existing bar joists were left exposed, as were roof beams and support columns.

LEFT: The second-floor porch was retained, although the railings and the roof were replaced.

HERON HAUS

CONSTRUCTION TYPE:
Site Built

ARCHITECT/BUILDER:
Tessa Smith,
Artisans Group

PHOTOGRAPHER:
Poppi Photography

LOCATION:
Olympia, Wash.

SIZE:
1,100 sq. ft.

DONNA AND STEVE MOVED BACK TO WASHINGTON
State from New Zealand for Donna's new job. The couple was looking to live in a community close to Seattle with small town charm, and they also wanted to be near to aging parents and friends.

New Zealand is a country that is highly advanced when it comes to sustainable building and Passive House (PH) construction, so it was no surprise that Donna and Steve would seek out sustainable options for their new home in the U.S. A side benefit of a sustainable home is lower utility bills. They wanted the house to have a clean, industrial look, and they weren't interested in spending time maintaining a large house. The house would be built for aging in place, with features such as a curbless shower and an accessible kitchen. Their research brought them to Artisans Group, and they began the design process with them while they were still living in New Zealand.

DOWNSIZING BETWEEN COUNTRIES

Donna and Steve had renovated a 1907 house in another part of Seattle before they moved to New Zealand, where they rented several houses over the years. In both countries, the houses were much larger than the one they ultimately decided to build. Donna says they have never acquired huge amounts of stuff, and they've purged their belongings with each move back and forth from New Zealand. A long-time minimalist, she says she likes her homes to be "borderline austere," so with their return they didn't bring very much back with them.

Donna maintains a one-bedroom condo on Bainbridge Island for work and put most of her old furnishings there and bought new furnishings for the house. In the future, Donna says she plans to retire and live in the Olympia house full time. The screened porch is designed as a potential phase two master suite when that time comes. The couple isn't certain they'll convert the space since they like the screened porch and don't find the house too small as it is. However, the phase two potential provides space to dream. The only time they'd like the extra space now is when company comes and they have to "camp" in the Volkswagen Westfalia inside the garage or stay at rented accommodations.

Although Donna and Steve don't have an excessive amount of possessions, they like a clean and tidy appearance, so storage was a priority in the small house. According to Donna, "The walk-in closet in the bedroom, the linen closet in the bath, and space for storage racks in the garage make it work."

Everything from how the home is situated on the lot to its floor plan and the roof's pitch is designed to work with natural light for warmth and coziness during the winter months without overheating in the summer. The roof is standing-seam metal, which is highly sustainable and environmentally friendly; it is also solar-panel ready.

ABOVE: To give the house the clean industrial appearance that Donna and Steve desired, a duct for the heat recovery ventilator is exposed in the living and kitchen area. The kitchen was designed to be sleek and modern but also accessible.

RIGHT: The massive sliding doors and clerestory windows in the living room offer optimal solar exposure while bringing in ample light and expanding the feel of the small floor plan.

FOREVER KITCHEN DESIGN

Because kitchens are such an important part of the house, they should be designed both for now and for the future. Some of the design features that make the kitchen in Heron Haus viable for the long term are:

- upper cabinets at an easily accessible height
- lower cabinets with drawers for easy access
- pullout drawers in pantries
- rounded edges on countertops
- appliances at or below eye level
- adequate clearance space around the kitchen
- slip-resistant floors

For more detailed information about making kitchens more universally accessible, visit ada.gov/ada_intro.htm.

The flooring in most of the house is polished concrete, which offers a clean, modern look and also functions as thermal mass to keep the house warm in winter and cool in summer.

ABOVE: The bedroom can be opened to the office space beyond with pocket doors on either side of the bed. There is a second office (not shown) that is sized as a single bedroom and could be used as a guest room in the future.

LEFT: The narrow office space gets extra light from the interior clerestory window.

DOWNSIZING FEATURES
- Built small (with the possibility for expansion)
- One-floor living
- Barrier-free shower
- Upper kitchen cabinets built low
- Roll-out drawers
- Lots of storage
- High ceilings
- Daylighting
- Flex space

GREEN FEATURES
- Heat recovery ventilator (HRV)
- LED lights
- Concrete floors
- Heat pump

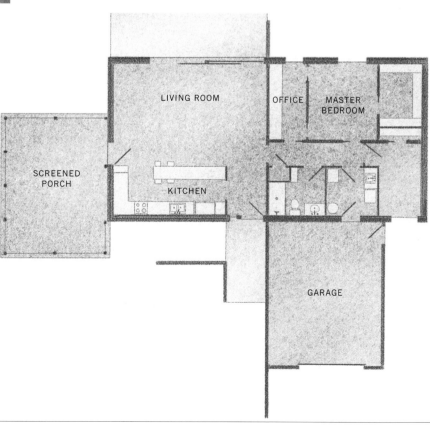

ABOVE LEFT: The concrete elements at the entry create a courtyard effect and become a backdrop for dramatic plantings while framing a strong relationship between the house and the site.

ABOVE RIGHT: The concrete "spine" continues inside, forming one wall of the living room and entry and visually connecting the interior with the exterior.

LEFT: The house was designed so the screened-in porch could some-day become a master bedroom if the owners ever decide they want to expand the house.

BUILDING THE HOUSE

The couple decided to build the house to meet many of the PH standards because they wanted it to be as efficient as possible, but they decided not to have it certified. For one reason, the water-heating option they chose was unlikely to meet certification requirements. And designing the house with the possibility of future expansion also complicates the issue of PH certification.

One of the defining features of the house is the use of concrete, with concrete flooring throughout the interior and a concrete "spine" that is continuous from the exterior through to the interior. The exposed concrete is visible on the exterior in the photo at top left and on the interior in the photo above right. The concrete also forms one wall of the shower.

LAKE SUPERIOR HOUSE

CONSTRUCTION TYPE:
Site Built/Structural
Insulated Panels (SIPs)

ARCHITECT:
McMonigal Architects

PHOTOGRAPHER:
Greg Page Photography

LOCATION:
Cornucopia, Wisc.

SIZE:
1,500 sq. ft.

IN 2016, ANN AND PETE BROWNLEE WERE LIVING IN a 2,600-sq.-ft. farmhouse built in 1992 on 10 acres. As empty nesters, they decided that the house (and its outbuildings and surrounding land) was more than they wanted to care for in the future. They were looking forward to simplifying their lives and building a home close to nature that would fit their current and future needs.

Ann and Pete have a strong attachment to the area along the south shore of Lake Superior; Pete's grandmother lived in Cornucopia in her retirement years, and Pete visited her there in his youth—and next door to the site is a cabin owned by the family. The couple enjoy the quiet woods, the sandy beaches, the beautiful bay, and the dirt roads in the area.

The new home is on a site that is heavily wooded and slightly sloping from the road with a steep bank down to the lake. The house fits in a narrow zone defined by lake and road setbacks with its natural beauty preserved by virtue of minimal disturbance to the site. With their respect for the land, the couple built floating wood paths so as not to disturb the natural grasses, and the land surrounding the house was left untouched.

As they made plans to sell their larger house, the couple's goal was to get rid of things they didn't need: They had been gradually giving away items to their adult children and nieces and nephews. The new house would have more built-ins, contemporary furniture, and a smaller scale; they wanted quality over quantity and were willing to sacrifice space to get it. As Ann says, "I love having just enough and everything I need in the house."

DESIGNING THE NEW HOME

The couple contacted architect Rosemary McMonigal, who has a reputation for designing energy-efficient homes. McMonigal incorporated all of the technology and research she has discovered over the years to make this house as energy efficient and sustainable as possible. She started with a grid and designed all of the rooms within it, eliminating unnecessary spaces such as hallways and alcoves.

The house they built is considerably smaller than their old house, one that requires less maintenance and less energy to operate. Almost all of the furniture is new and lighter—visually appropriate for the space and in contrast to the bulky, more traditional furniture in their former house. A couple of Danish modern teak side tables that belonged to Ann's parents fit right in. Pete and Ann made the dining table together out of old-growth flame birch that was recovered from the bottom of Lake Superior. In their bedroom is the bed that Pete made when they married.

In contrast to the "buttoned-up" front façade, the back side of the house opens up to a backyard of low-maintenance natural grasses and prairie flowers.

ABOVE: Concrete floors and walls and vertical steel rods at the stairs (see also p. 111) contribute to the spare, rugged quality of the open-plan interior. Radiant-floor heating, supplemented by a woodstove, keeps the house feeling warm and requires minimal energy.

LEFT: The modern Scandinavian furnishings reflect the homeowners' desire for simplicity in this, their forever home. The wood-paneled wall in the rear of the living room, made from reclaimed barn wood, serves as a focal point, its color and texture countering the otherwise neutral palette.

FACING PAGE TOP: The bedrooms have generous windows that bring in light and ventilation.

FACING PAGE BOTTOM: The cozy bunkroom provides overflow sleeping accommodations for out-of-town guests and family.

BUILDING FOR ENERGY EFFICIENCY

The house was built as efficiently as possible with minimal waste and using recycled materials wherever feasible. The countertops in the kitchen and bathrooms are of 75% recycled materials, such as glass, mirror, and earthenware and vitrified ash. And the feature wall in the living room was designed with reclaimed barn wood.

The house has a superinsulated envelope with continuously insulated concrete mass walls and foundation and a structural insulated panel (SIP) roof (see the sidebar on p. 154). The insulated concrete walls and floor are not only efficient but also provide the advantage of thermal mass. Radiant-floor heating keeps the house comfortably warm and costs less to operate over the long run than many other heating and cooling systems. Careful placement of windows promotes cross-ventilation. With deep overhangs around the periphery of the house, air conditioning is not required. Ample daylighting reduces the use of light fixtures and electricity.

McMonigal says there are lessons to be learned from the construction of this house: "A relaxing retreat does not need to be oversized to rejuvenate one's senses; simple forms and materials help a building blend into its surroundings. The small size works wonderfully when well designed, and natural beauty can best be preserved by decisions that lessen the disturbance to the site."

DOWNSIZING FEATURES
- High ceilings
- Minimal hallways
- Low-maintenance materials
- Open floor plan
- Fewer bathrooms to save space, cost, and maintenance
- Right-size rooms
- Multipurpose spaces
- Screened porch bridges interior to exterior without more house space
- Lots of outdoor spaces

GREEN FEATURES
- Superinsulated
- Structural insulated panel (SIPs) roof
- Concrete-sandwich walls for thermal mass
- High-efficiency windows
- Large overhangs
- Indigenous landscaping
- Low-VOC finishes
- Daylighting
- No air conditioning
- Standing-seam roof
- Repurposed and recycled materials
- Locally sourced materials

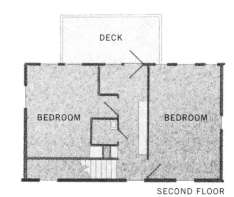

DECK

BEDROOM

BEDROOM

SECOND FLOOR

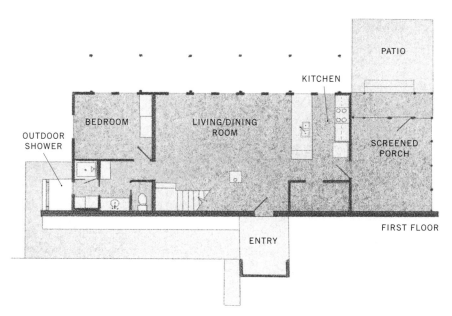

PATIO

KITCHEN

OUTDOOR
SHOWER

BEDROOM

LIVING/DINING
ROOM

SCREENED
PORCH

FIRST FLOOR

ENTRY

The metal rods add a beautiful industrial design feature while creating minimal separation between the stairs and the rest of the room.

Tall concrete walls shield the house and porch from prevailing west winds while providing privacy from the road.

OPEN FLOOR PLANS

At one time, most houses were built with discrete spaces for the kitchen, dining room, and living room areas. Today, however, most people prefer an open plan for the common areas, where all of these rooms are connected to each other with fewer partition walls. Sometimes referred to as a "great" room, this space allows flexibility in design and ready communication between rooms. When one person is cooking, he or she can talk with family members or guests relaxing in the living room. An open plan also eliminates the need for hallways that are wasted space.

Open floor plans allow for an easier flow of air and light through the space, minimizing the need for artificial ventilation and lighting. They are also particularly advantageous for older people who can get around more easily without having to negotiate barrier walls. Some people create divisions within the space using a kitchen island as a divider or color changes, moldings, ceiling lights, and materials that define the areas without walls.

ABOVE: The brown and gray color palette of cedar siding and concrete walls mimics the colors of tree trunks and rock outcroppings in the surrounding area. The exterior of the house is super-insulated with a concrete wall envelope that was poured and insulated on site; highly energy-efficient structural insulated panels (SIPs) were used for the roof.

LEFT: Wood walkways appear to float above the ground, leaving the forest floor undisturbed. An outside shower is tucked behind the wall at left, providing an added place for guests to shower in summer (the house has only one bathroom).

WEE BARN

CONSTRUCTION TYPE:
Modular/Panelized

ARCHITECT/PROJECT
MANAGER:
Geoffrey C. Warner,
Alchemy Architects

GENERAL CONTRACTOR:
Carina Construction

MANUFACTURER:
Apex Homes

PHOTOGRAPHER:
Geoffrey C. Warner

LOCATION:
Corning, N.Y.

SIZE:
1,436 sq. ft.

ROBIN WAS IN THE PROCESS OF TRANSITIONING from a position in urban digital arts administration to retirement when she decided to build herself a forever home. She sought a modest home in a picturesque pasture in rural upstate New York. Her priorities for the space included a place to practice her own art, host guests, and age in place gracefully. The house she built manages to be modern in technology and traditional, industrial, and handcrafted in design, while also cozy with adequate flex space.

Prior to moving to Corning she lived in Minneapolis in a 2,000-sq.-ft. 1920s bungalow. The move wasn't just a matter of downsizing but more a change in how she wanted to live her life, embracing many of the things that were previously hobbies or dreams. On her ten acres she keeps chickens, ducks, and bees. She works part-time in a tasting room at a Finger Lakes vineyard and on a small farm as a "junior naturalist." Since she has lived in her new house she has gone to taxidermy school, carpentry school for women (where she built a chicken coop), and has twice attended Cornell's Spring Field Ornithology program. Robin cooks a lot for herself and friends. She says, "I still work as a museum consultant and teach online in Johns Hopkins Master of Arts Museum Studies program, but my hobbies and interests have moved to the center of my life, something that seemed impossible in Minneapolis where the focus was my career."

DOWNSIZING FROM CITY TO COUNTRY

Downsizing from 2,000 sq. ft. to just over 1,400 sq. ft. was less about square footage than configuration. Robin's Minneapolis house had three floors, made up of relatively small rooms, while her new house is mostly on one open level, with little separation between spaces in the main "box," which contains all of the common rooms including the main living area and bedroom/bath. Reducing her material possessions to what is important and necessary turned into a larger philosophical way of living and the way she now wants to conduct her life. As she says, "Virtually everything in my possession now has provenance and meaning; I'm done with unnecessary chattel." Although aging in place was not her major focus, she says this home will be an easy one to grow old in.

Architect Geoffrey Warner designed the house so that although it is small, all of the space is well used. There are no hallways and no wasted space. There is a studio and guest loft in the barn area, so Robin can do her own artwork and be able to host guests.

The three sections of the house are defined by the siding, with the main house sided in a corrugated weathering steel, the garage in black corrugated steel, and the barn in the center in rough-sawn pine locally sourced in random thicknesses and widths (and painted black). This creates a beautiful juxtaposition in color and shape between the three sections. These simple structures are built with modern technology but evoke a sense of timelessness that fits in with the agrarian location.

MINIMIZING ENERGY USE

The house was built so that air conditioning would not be necessary and mechanical heat would be kept to a minimum. In-floor hydronic heat with a dual-purpose condensing boiler and a woodstove maintain a comfortable temperature in the house, even on cold winter days. Exterior insulation forms a thermal break combined with a rain screen that voids the need for air conditioning. The house was designed to maximize the outdoor space and flawlessly integrate it with the interior space. Courtyards are created at the front of the house as well as to the side, with outside space also available at the front of the barn area.

From Warner's perspective, Robin's project posed some unique challenges. There was the creation of a modestly scaled house, on a tight budget, and with the small structures forming an intimate, protected outdoor space. They also needed to make the most of a prefabricated process, which limits building widths to about 16 ft. Even though the house is small, it manages to live larger than it is, with lots of daylight and varied views. It's a home created with simplicity but rich in design.

ABOVE: The main part of the house is open, with living room, dining, and kitchen blending into each other. A woodstove supplements the hydronic radiant heating system, keeping the house warm without using a lot of energy.

RIGHT: The kitchen cabinets are from IKEA and the countertops are made from Richlite, a recycled paper product that is durable and sustainable.

CORRUGATED WEATHERING STEEL

Weathering-type steel combines alloys that are meant to develop a rust exterior, which acts as a protective coating if the material is left untreated and exposed to the elements. Its surface layer, or patina, protects it from further corrosion. Weathering steel is often referred to by the trademark COR-TEN steel, which is manufactured by U.S. Steel.

Weathering steel exhibits increased resistance to atmospheric corrosion compared to other types of steel and eliminates the need for painting and rust-prevention maintenance. Exposure to humid subtropical climates or water pooling on the steel may destabilize the coating, however, leading to corrosion. Corrugated weathering steel is best used in a dry environment and on a structure with adequate drainage.

DOWNSIZING FEATURES
- Easy-access rooms
- Ramp to front door

GREEN FEATURES
- In-floor hydronic heat
- Woodstove
- Condensing boiler
- Permeable paving
- Local materials
- Low-flow faucets and showers
- Dual-flush toilet
- Low- or no-VOC paints
- Natural landscaping
- LED lighting
- No air conditioning
- Detached garage

The back side of the home is punctuated by four windows, which provide a good deal of natural light and views to the surrounding horse pasture.

ABOVE AND LEFT: The barn area includes a lofted bedroom and studio space for guests. The loft area was panelized, which was more cost-efficient here than using modular construction, as in the rest of the house.

RIVERVIEW HOUSE

CONSTRUCTION TYPE:
Site Built

ARCHITECT:
Alterstudio Architecture

PHOTOGRAPHER:
Casey Dunn

LOCATION:
Austin, Tex.

SIZE:
1,875 sq. ft.

FOR 25 YEARS, THE OWNERS LIVED IN A 2,500-SQ.-FT. house built in the 1960s in a neighborhood of Austin. Although they made renovations during their time there, it was never going to be the modern house they aspired to. So when their children graduated from college, they decided it was time to move and downsize closer to the city center.

Choosing the lot was the most difficult part of the process, and it took the couple almost two years to find the perfect site. They wanted to be within close biking distance of both of their jobs, and even closer to restaurants and parks. At first, they were hesitant about purchasing the lot they finally chose because it was so small and narrow (41 ft. by 155 ft.). But they reconsidered because it met their other criteria, with a location next door to one of Austin's largest parks. Ultimately, they asked Alterstudio if they could design a house for the lot, despite its size and shape, and the architectural firm was up for the challenge.

DOWNSIZING ROOM BY ROOM

Like so many couples, after 25 years in their family house, they had accumulated a lot of things they realized they no longer needed. When construction started on their new house, and they expected that moving was about a year away, they started cleaning out their old house. They methodically started sorting through items to keep and those they would donate, sell, give away, or trash. They went from closet to closet, room by room, to the attic and garage. As the owner says, "We took a long, patient approach."

The owners recommend to others that they downsize sooner rather than later so they can enjoy their new home for a longer time and not have to worry about doing it in the future. Living in a smaller house with less upkeep allows more time for fun!

WORKING WITH ALTERSTUDIO ARCHITECTURE

The owners didn't have an exhaustive list of must-haves for this new house. Important features were lots of light and energy efficiency. Having indoor/outdoor space became a top priority during the later stages of design, and they did insist on having a sliding door with a 10-ft. opening connecting the living space with the front yard. Otherwise, they relied on the expertise of Alterstudio to guide them through the design and construction.

The original design for the house had two stories, but after getting an estimate well over the homeowners' budget, Alterstudio redesigned the house with just one floor. The owners say this plan is much better for

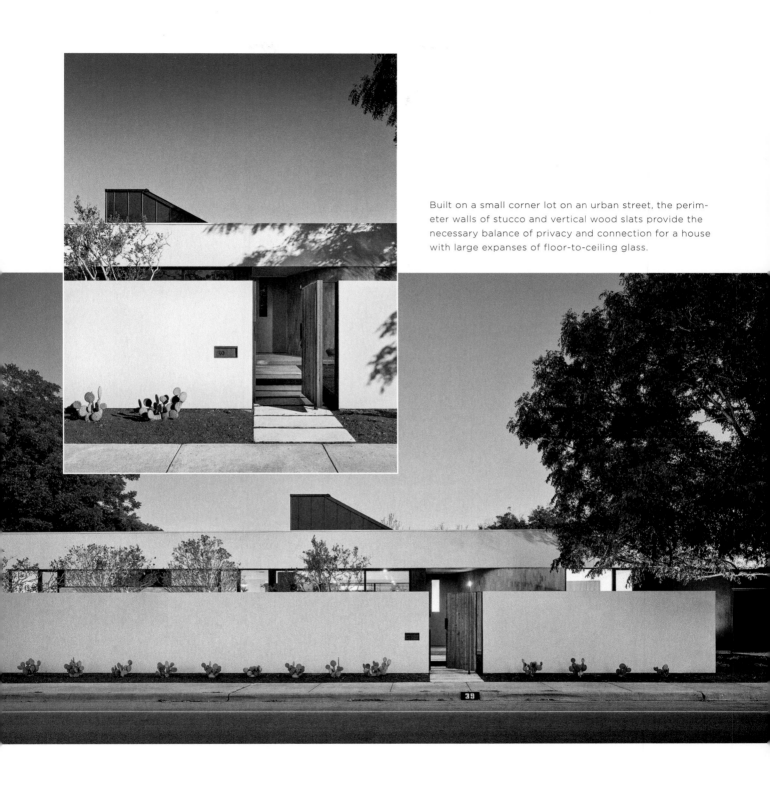

Built on a small corner lot on an urban street, the perimeter walls of stucco and vertical wood slats provide the necessary balance of privacy and connection for a house with large expanses of floor-to-ceiling glass.

ONE-FLOOR LIVING

Many homeowners, both young and old, are opting for single-story living. Understandably, baby boomers are especially concerned with possible unforeseen eventualities, such as broken bones or age-related issues dealing with climbing stairs. Many domestic injuries occur on the stairs of a home, and, in case of fire, escape is easier from a single-story house.

The cost of energy can also be lower, with air circulating more easily. Design possibilities are enhanced with one-story living. Staircases can take up space that can be more efficiently used, vaulted ceilings and skylights are easier to create, and a more open plan is possible with fewer supporting walls in a single-story home.

ABOVE: White oak flooring is used throughout the house including the kitchen, where the complementary rift-sawn white oak cabinets provide plenty of storage and also enclose space for two refrigerator and freezer units.

BELOW: The master bedroom has a view to the side yard, with privacy to the corner street provided by the wood-slat fence. The ceiling fan provides cool air to supplement the air conditioning.

A wall of glass connects the living room to a private courtyard, which is screened from the street by the stucco wall. Most of the furniture came from their previous house, including the mid-century modern sofa.

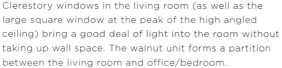

Clerestory windows in the living room (as well as the large square window at the peak of the high angled ceiling) bring a good deal of light into the room without taking up wall space. The walnut unit forms a partition between the living room and office/bedroom.

them for many reasons—for one, avoiding steps will likely be beneficial as they grow older. They did not intentionally design for aging, but their architect and their builder did, with a rimless shower in the master bathroom, space to add a shower seat, and accommodation for the addition of grab bars in the future.

LIVING WITH LESS SPACE

In contrast to their previous home, where several rooms sat unused once the owners' daughters had moved away, almost every space in their new home is used every day. They don't miss the extra spaces or the yard maintenance required now that they just have a half-acre lawn. They have a spacious

city park next door—which they do not have to maintain, of course. They can comfortably accommodate overnight visitors in the guest bedroom and the office, which converts into a second guest bedroom.

The house's 28 solar panels and a variable refrigerant flow (VRF) heating and cooling system have helped the owners save energy. (VRF is an HVAC system that uses refrigerant as the cooling and heating vehicle and supports both ducted and ductless air distribution configurations.) During the first year in their house, they generated almost the same amount of energy they used, with the electric portion of their utilities bill virtually zero.

Their landscaping is with drought-tolerant plantings, tailored to the local climate. Because their lot is so small and their plantings require minimal water, the water bill is significantly lower than it was at their previous home.

The house is perfect for entertaining guests both inside and outdoors with a table and grill on the patio. But the owners say it is also just right for the two of them, plus their dog Mojo, when they are not entertaining. The living room/office spaces make it comfortable for them to do things independently (work/read/watch television) while still in each other's company.

During the design and building stages, Alterstudio would sometimes suggest architectural features that would increase the resale value of the home. Their response was always the same: "We're building this house for us. We aren't going to sell it."

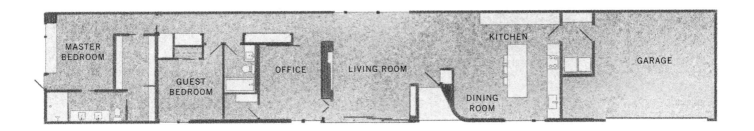

MULTIPURPOSE ROOMS

To make the best use of space in a home, it is preferable if some of the rooms in the house are multipurpose. At one time, living rooms and dining rooms were formal, used only for entertaining. Kitchens were just for cooking and eating, and bedrooms were just for sleeping. Today, many houses are designed with rooms that can be used for multiple purposes. In the Riverview House, for example, the flex space can be used as an office, reading area, or extra bedroom when one is required.

One of the keys to living in a small house is using the spaces to the greatest benefit. Many of the people interviewed for this book said they enjoyed being able to utilize every inch of space in their homes, which is enhanced by having a multi-purpose room.

DOWNSIZING FEATURES
- One-floor living
- Lots of storage
- Multipurpose rooms
- Barrier-free shower
- Large windows
- High ceiling
- Lots of light

GREEN FEATURES
- Net positive (the house produces more energy than it consumes)
- Solar panels
- LED lighting
- Ceiling fans
- ENERGY STAR appliances
- Native plantings
- Low water use

ABOVE: The sliding glass doors to the living area extend the house into the outdoor space. The panel midway down the window wall is glazed tile, which affords privacy to the guest bedroom and office.

LEFT: The folding door on the end of the walnut unit can be closed to separate the living room from the flex room beyond when the couple converts the office to an extra bedroom. (This is the view from inside the flex space; the saffron-colored couch opens to a bed.)

A HOME IN FLETCHER PLACE

CONSTRUCTION TYPE:
Site Built

ARCHITECT/BUILDER:
ONE 10 STUDIO
Architects

PHOTOGRAPHER:
Lesle Lane, Studio 13
Photography

LOCATION:
Indianapolis, Ind.

SIZE:
1,437 sq. ft.

FACING PAGE: Building a new house in an established neighborhood has its challenges. It was important to integrate the modern exterior appearance of the new home with the traditional character of the neighborhood. Horizontal cedar cladding on the façade provides a visual connection with the neighboring houses, and the covered entryway adds a familiar note of welcome.

AS AN INDIANAPOLIS REALTOR, JOE HAD LOOKED AT thousands of houses during his career, so he knew exactly what he wanted for his own new home. In the established Fletcher Place neighborhood of Indianapolis, he purchased a 33-ft.-wide infill lot bordered by a public street and alleys on three of its boundaries. There he decided to build a compact, efficient contemporary residence, with a modest footprint and a limited project budget.

MOVING FROM LARGE TO SMALL

Joe's prior residence was in the northern suburbs of Indianapolis, in Carmel, which he shared with his then wife and their four children. Their 3,600-sq.-ft. house had five bedrooms, spaces for televisions, study areas, and a formal dining room. With a good deal of space and a big yard, there was a "ridiculous amount of maintenance," according to Joe. In addition, he says he had to drive everywhere, with nothing in walking distance. He also claims his electric bills were extremely high.

When Joe split up with his wife, he decided he no longer wanted a large house and all the work required to maintain it. In addition, Joe's kids were getting older and weren't around very often; he therefore had no use for extra bedrooms and other rooms that were never going to be used except for gathering dust. There was no need for a formal living or dining room that would be used perhaps once a year. Joe reflected on the spaces he did use on a daily basis, which included only a bedroom, a bathroom, an office, a media space, a kitchen/eating area, and a garage. He decided these spaces didn't need to be large, just functional.

Weary of huge energy bills, he wanted to minimize energy use, maximize efficiency, and not pay to heat/cool rooms that he wasn't going to use every day. Minimizing maintenance was another priority. Joe and his architectural team chose materials that were low maintenance, such as the brick, steel, and cedar on the exterior of the house. Aside from caulking window and door gaps and resealing the cedar every few years, Joe says, the exterior is virtually maintenance-free.

Being in the real estate business, Joe often has conversations with people of all ages who are moving and dealing with mounds of belongings. He definitely sees a trend toward minimizing and simplifying, which he believes is not just a fad. As Joe observes, "Large groups of consumers and homeowners are coming to terms with a culture and society that tell us that acquiring more material possessions is a sign of success and happiness." He feels that more space and more stuff actually means less time and less happiness in the long run. "Time spent caring for, cleaning, main-

taining, repairing, and curating all of our collections and the spaces required to store them—our homes and storage spaces—is time *not* spent caring for ourselves, each other, and our communities."

WORKING WITH THE ARCHITECT

After Joe's first few meetings seeing some initial sketches, it was clear to him that ONE 10 STUDIO understood his concept and intention for this house. Architects Patrick Kestner and Clete Kunce of ONE 10 STUDIO took the time to learn about Joe, how he lived, the spaces he desired and needed, and those that were unnecessary and unwanted. They designed the house to suit Joe's needs, not their architectural vision of what they wanted to design.

Joe credits ONE 10 STUDIO for the extremely efficient design. There is hardly a square foot of the house that he doesn't use on a daily basis and no wasted, single-use space. As an example, he cites the lack of hallways in the upper level, with stairs going directly into his bedroom. Walk-in closets were eliminated in favor of floor-to-ceiling wardrobes, permitting that space to be used for something more functional. The bedroom on the

ABOVE AND RIGHT: The kitchen, dining area, and living area are essentially one large room. Other than the brick, carried inside from the exterior façade, and the dark walnut frame between the entry hall and kitchen, almost all of the interior is white.

main level was purposefully designed to serve as a dual-purpose room, functioning as a spare bedroom on the rare occasion that Joe has guests. All of his activities can be confined to the spaces designed for them, and there's not an extra spot that's underutilized or totally unused.

Kestner acknowledges that there were challenges delivering materials and erecting and completing the building on this compact urban site. However, he points out that this small modern residence demonstrates that quality architecture can happen at any scale and on any budget.

The home occupies a narrow 33-ft.-wide infill lot bordered by a public street and alleys on three sides.

INFILL LOTS

An infill lot is a single vacant property in a predominantly built-up area that is bounded on two or more sides by existing development and can be "filled in" with a new structure. The term can also refer to a lot containing an existing structure that will be removed and replaced with a new structure. Generally, utility supply lines are already in place, so bringing them to the site is not usually necessary. However, it is recommended that you have the existing utilities inspected for current code compliance and longevity. Infill lots are considered green because they contribute to neighborhood revitalization and increase density without adding additional infrastructure.

Some certification programs today offer points for building on infill lots.

With the demand for housing in established neighborhoods, infill lots may be the best or only alternative in a particular neighborhood. Often these lots are close to public transportation, shopping, and other amenities, making them ideal for people who desire a more urban environment, but one outside of the city. These types of sites often appeal to downsizers because they entail lower maintenance and cost, as well as less dependence on driving. The lots are typically small, also making them ideal for people seeking to build or remodel small houses.

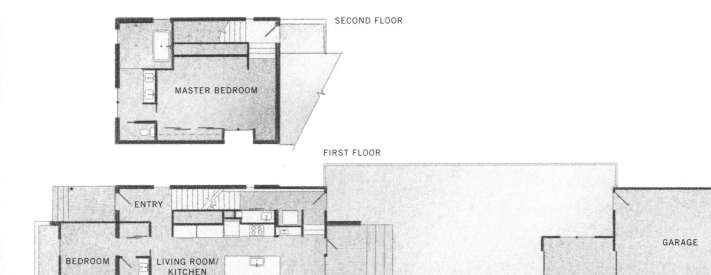

SECOND FLOOR

MASTER BEDROOM

FIRST FLOOR

ENTRY

BEDROOM

LIVING ROOM/
KITCHEN

GARAGE

DOWNSIZING FEATURES
- Wall-less and barrier-free shower
- Easy flow through the house
- Minimal hallways

GREEN FEATURES
- Low-flow faucets and showerheads
- Forest Stewardship Council (FSC)-certified wood
- Recycled metal
- ENERGY STAR appliances
- Infill lot
- Detached garage

Multiple openings on the back side of the house provide lots of natural light and ventilation, in contrast to the minimal windows on the front. A covered porch overlooking the back-yard extends the living area.

The garage is detached from the residence at the back of the house and is the homeowner's one concession to clutter. (As he says, "I do occasionally like to make a mess, and that couldn't happen in the pure white interior of my house.") The garage also houses his vintage Vespa.

TOP: Joe's upstairs master bedroom continues the monotone look of the rest of the house. The four opaque sliding glass doors to the closet echo the opaque panels on the back of the garage.

ABOVE: The stark all-white bathroom has an open, rimless shower and modern freestanding bathtub in keeping with the contemporary aesthetic of the house.

THE COTTAGE AT EXTOWN FARM

CONSTRUCTION TYPE:
Site Built

ARCHITECT:
David Harlan, David D. Harlan Architects

LOCATION:
New Canaan, Conn.

SIZE:
1,450 sq. ft.

THE COTTAGE AT EXTOWN FARM, LOCATED ON A historic site in New Canaan, Conn., was once part of a large farm developed in the 1700s. The owner purchased 17 acres with a small caretaker's cottage and a very run-down main house on the property, along with a barn and surrounding farmland. His intent was to remodel the small caretaker's cottage to live in while he rebuilt the main house.

Before buying this property, the owner lived with his wife and four children in a 10,000-sq.-ft. estate on a 30-acre horse farm in Greenwich. After years of marriage, he got divorced and his children were out of the house, living on their own. When he married his second wife, he decided to sell the large estate, and together they chose property in New Canaan, a quintessential New England town that was close to his business in Greenwich. They called on architect David Harlan to design the small cottage on the property for them to live in temporarily, until they were ready to rebuild the main house. However, after living in the cottage for some time, they liked it so much they decided they wanted to stay there.

MAINTAINING HISTORICAL CHARACTER

Because of the historic nature of the property, Harlan was required to reference and preserve the character of the farm's protected status. The existing scale, form, massing, color, operable divided-lite windows, material textures, shingles, copper gutters, stonework, and carpentry details dictated the design of the small cottage. The new front porch was allowed as a complementary addition to the farm's visual appearance.

It was also required that the cottage be in the same location as it was prior to the rebuild, though they were allowed to reorient the structure to take the best advantage of solar gain. The entry drive was shifted away from the cottage, creating a new meadow and parking area by the barn. Paving stones were added from the barn to the porch entry.

DOWNSIZING FROM VERY BIG TO VERY SMALL

Moving from a 10,000-sq.-ft. house to a 1,450-sq.-ft. cottage meant there were lots of furnishings, clothing, books, and other items to dispose of in order for the couple to move into the much smaller space. The owner offered his children whatever they might want for their own homes and gave a good deal of what remained to Goodwill. He and his wife made a conscious effort to get rid of as much stuff as possible. Because the owner had transitioned from a job in Manhattan where he had to wear suits and ties every day to his business in Greenwich that had a more casual dress code, there were lots of clothes that could be disposed of. Downsizing

From the outside, the house appears to have two stories but it is just one story with high ceilings, which gives the house a more spacious feel than the petite plan would suggest. The entry drive was shifted away from the cottage, gently curving around a grass meadow and ending in the new barn area, where there is parking.

LEFT: The central multipurpose space, open to the kitchen, is flooded with natural light from the clerestory windows at ceiling level. The hand-painted mural over the fireplace, reminiscent of an earlier, pastoral time, depicts renovations and additions to the original main house on the property.

BELOW: The east-facing sunroom carries the color scheme and wood paneling from the interior living space and also shares the fireplace. The door at the far end leads to the front porch.

was a revelation for the couple—and a lesson that in the future they should only buy what they need.

A COMFORTABLE PLAN

The design of the cottage perfectly accommodates the couple's new downsized life. Having multiple areas where they could sit either together or alone was crucial to their comfort. With a closed-in sunroom, outside porch, bedroom sitting area, and living room, there are four distinct areas to sit, read, dine, or relax. The fireplace is two-sided (with hearths in the living room and in the sunroom), which means two people can either enjoy the fire sitting side by side or separately in two different rooms. In terms of clothes storage, Harlan designed a large dressing room with ample cabinets and hanging space for husband and wife, so storage would not be an issue, particularly for their pared-down life.

Living in this small house, the owner says he feels more connected to the outdoors. He's more apt to take a walk, work on his large vegetable garden, or experience some of what the town has to offer. He says their life is more balanced between home, leisure time, and work. They love living in a smaller space and are much happier today with less.

The wide plank floors, wood paneling, and light olive color scheme contribute to the warm, cozy feel of the living area.

HIGH CEILINGS

High ceilings can be a positive way to create a more spacious home and an excellent method for the downsizer to use in adjusting to a smaller space. The height gives the rooms a sense of spaciousness that belies the actual footprint of the house. In recent years, standard ceilings have gone from 8 ft. to 9 ft., with many custom homes designed with a vaulted ceiling in at least one room. People who want to give the house a more expansive feel will increase ceiling heights for the entire house, as was accomplished with the 16-ft. ceilings in The Cottage at Extown Farm.

By contrast, low ceilings can create a feeling of being cramped and less accommodating, though sometimes they are cozier. This can be rectified in a house with the use of color, décor, and windows.

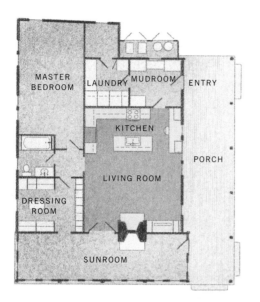

MASTER BEDROOM

LAUNDRY MUDROOM ENTRY

KITCHEN

PORCH

LIVING ROOM

DRESSING ROOM

SUNROOM

The gracious porch runs along the north side of the house, which overlooks the red barn and stone walls of the yard. The porch's overhang and the surrounding trees provide welcome shade during the warmer months.

DOWNSIZING FEATURES
- Multipurpose rooms
- Master bedroom on first floor
- Flexibility for shifting needs
- Multiple sitting areas
- Extensive outdoor space

GREEN FEATURES
- Optimal solar orientation
- Natural ventilation
- High-efficiency HVAC
- Double-glazed windows
- Low-VOC paints
- Recycled materials
- Recycled cabinetry from original house
- ENERGY STAR appliances
- Reused portion of foundation
- Recycled waste

The red barn in the background, one of the original structures on the property, is now home to a rustic indoor basketball court.

The original caretaker's house on this historic 17-acre estate was built in the 1930s. Some of the original foundation and wall framing was used for the new cottage. The details, materials, and form were modeled after other buildings on the property.

SOLTERRE CONCEPT HOUSE

CONSTRUCTION TYPE:
Site Built

ARCHITECT:
Solterre Design

PHOTOGRAPHER:
Adam Cornick, Acorn Art & Photography

LOCATION:
Nova Scotia, Canada

SIZE:
1,500 sq. ft.

CERTIFICATIONS:
LEED for Homes Platinum

Passive House

ONE PART DEMONSTRATION SITE FOR THE COUPLE'S architectural firm (Solterre Design) and one part future retirement home, the Solterre Concept House currently serves as a weekend home and rental unit, while the architect-owners live in a 125-year-old farmhouse in Halifax. The two houses are roughly the same size, but the similarities end there. Downsizing isn't only about building smaller but also about scaling back on energy consumption. The off-the-grid Solterre Concept House is a model of energy efficiency compared to the farmhouse, as well as being greener, more affordable to operate and maintain, and more comfortable to live in.

Jennifer Corson and Keith Robertson, husband and wife architect-owners, fell in love with the Lunenburg area after designing several homes there for clients. A lot came up for sale on a saltwater inlet on Second Peninsula that had difficult access to power, so they decided it was a great spot to build their off-the-grid highly energy-efficient weekend house. Designing it on one level meant it would be excellent for future aging in place when they moved into the house full time. So what is now a second home, was planned from the start as a "forever home."

BUILDING OFF-THE-GRID

Designing the house to be off-the-grid involved some difficult planning for which Jennifer and Keith received lots of help from their colleagues. It was also a challenge to meet the stringent standards of both LEED for Homes and Passive House certification. They were at a huge advantage, however, because their firm had already designed many high-performance houses over the years and they were familiar with all of the products that went into the assembly of the foundation, roof, and walls. They used triple-glazed windows. Overhangs on the east and west sides minimize potential overheating. Thermal mass from the concrete floors helps keep the house cool in the warm months and warm in the colder months.

The house is not tied to the grid but receives all of its electricity through the photovoltaic (PV) panels on the roof of the utility shed. Primary heat is supplied by solar energy, both passive and active, along with a small high-efficiency woodstove. Solar thermal panels supply heat for hot water and secondary heating. Propane fuels the kitchen stove and acts as a supplementary backup fuel to the heat and hot-water systems. A DC refrigerator and other ENERGY STAR appliances were installed because every kilowatt of energy used has to be produced on site. By using the most energy-efficient lighting, appliances, and equipment possible, the number of PV panels required is relatively small, making off-the-grid living

Located on a saltwater inlet on Second Peninsula, Nova Scotia, the house is off-the-grid, with heat for hot water and secondary heating provided by the solar panels on the rear roof over the bedroom wing. The large windows with southern exposure, oriented for maximum active and passive solar gain, create much of the heating needed for the home.

The open kitchen and dining area features a reclaimed carved wood sign on the front of the kitchen island. All the cabinetry is salvaged, as is the 12-ft. stainless-steel countertop (which came from a convent in Halifax).

SALVAGED MATERIALS

Using salvaged materials helps preserve natural resources while limiting the amount of debris going into landfills. Reusing materials is also an opportunity to showcase some of our history and culture. Commonly discarded or unused items are now being preserved not only to reduce construction costs but also to recreate historical architectural features in homes. Salvaged materials are available on many Internet sites and in stores around the country.

The Solterre Concept House contains numerous salvaged/reused materials, which include all the interior doors, the kitchen cabinets, countertops and sink, fireplace surround, some wall framing, and decommissioned acrylic store signage as shower surrounds. The salvage not only suits the owners' quirky aesthetic, but also adds history and character to their home. For more info about the owners' salvage company, visit: renovators-resource.com.

The unique tub/shower surround is a reclaimed acrylic sign, which adds a touch of whimsy to this eclectic master bathroom.

affordable while also exceptionally comfortable. (The home uses 70% to 90% less energy than a typical home of the same size.)

BEAUTIFUL HOUSE, IDEAL LOCATION

Jennifer and Keith agree that they couldn't have chosen a better location. They built the house on the upper edge of an established pasture, with full southern exposure. They access potable water from an artesian spring through a well dug just north of the house. The septic field, which uses recycled crushed bottle glass as an alternative to sand, is gravity-fed to the south. A shallow foundation system minimizes disruption to the land. Since the house is off-the-grid, the couple didn't have to cut any additional trees for power lines. There is a tree buffer to the north, east, and west, so the house is well protected from winter winds and any overheating issues in mornings or afternoons.

The headboard of the bed in the master bedroom is built from ornate Gothic wood panels that were once used to cover organ pipes. The base of the bed is from salvaged oak school desks from the recently closed Lunenburg Academy in the nearby town of Lunenburg, a UNESCO World Heritage Site.

ABOVE AND LEFT: Primary heat for the house is supplied by solar energy, both passive and active, with a small, high-efficiency Danish woodstove providing additional heat on cold winter days.

FACING PAGE TOP: All the reclaimed interior doors throughout the house came from the owners' salvage company, including the 12-ft.-tall rolling walnut doors that lead into the television room. The concrete floors with recycled-glass aggregate serve as thermal mass, helping to keep the house cool in summer and warm in winter.

FACING PAGE BOTTOM: The steep metal roof on the multifunctional utility shed houses the PV system, which is the electrical power source for the house.

According to Jennifer, "We love the connectedness to the sea, the closeness of a quaint, historically significant town, yet the quietness of the pasture and the woods. It really is picture perfect." The couple's two children (and their friends) also love to be at the Solterre Concept House. Jennifer and Keith built some outbuildings that are part of the charm of living there. The setting, on historic pastureland, overlooking the inlet, facing due south, is hard to beat in any season.

As well as being the architects, the owners are also partners in Renovators Resource in Halifax, which has been the supply house for salvaged materials for many of their company's projects (see the sidebar on p. 140). In this house, quirky salvaged materials bring a lot of whimsy and color to the home, capturing the past while embracing some new technology.

The large covered porch in the front of the house offers a cool place for dining. A wood slat screen of torrefied wood (see the sidebar on the facing page) encloses the porch. The wing wall to the right of the entry is salvaged acrylic, which illuminates as a nighttime entrance light.

The living roof over the entry side provides additional insulation (and helps the house blend in with its natural environment).

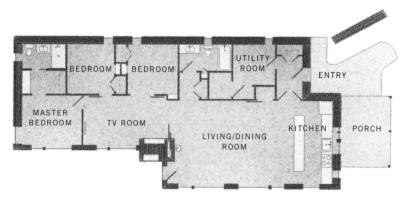

DOWNSIZING FEATURES
- No hallways
- Expansive windows
- Multipurpose rooms
- One-level living
- Vaulted ceiling giving illusion of more space
- Pocket doors (option to subdivide open-plan area)

GREEN FEATURES
- Salvaged materials
- Optimal solar orientation
- Rainwater cistern

- Recycled-glass/concrete foundation
- Living roof
- Superinsulated envelope
- Recycled newsprint insulation
- Heat recovery ventilator (HRV)
- Photovoltaic (PV) array
- Solar thermal panels
- Off-the-grid
- Large, south-facing windows
- High-efficiency appliances

The "Bull Shed" is a multipurpose outbuilding that provides overflow accommodations in the summer, a hangout for the owners' children, and storage space. It is built exclusively from salvaged materials.

TORREFIED WOOD

Torrefaction is a process whereby wood is put through a series of treatments that dry the wood and later add some moisture back into it. This creates an ecologically friendly, chemical-free, and rich colored wood (dependent on the species and treatment). If the wood is not treated with a UV protectant, the wood will turn a silver gray, requiring some maintenance. This technology provides an enhanced wood grain and creates a consistent color throughout the wood.

Torrefied wood is an attractive option for exterior applications because it is less likely to shrink, swell, or warp under harsh moisture conditions and is resistant to fungus and mold, which can degrade the wood. For further information check the website: thermalwoodcanada.com.

LIVE OAK HOUSE

CONSTRUCTION TYPE:
Site Built

ARCHITECT:
Rory Reynolds + Associates

PHOTOGRAPHER:
Mandy Cheng Design

LOCATION:
St. Augustine, Fla.

SIZE:
2,000 sq. ft.

CERTIFICATIONS:
LEED for Homes Platinum

Florida Green Building Coalition Platinum

Florida Water Star Gold

ENERGY STAR

USGBC Northeast Florida Green Home of the Year

COURTNEY OWNED A 4,000-SQ.-FT. HOUSE IN THE suburbs and was looking to purchase a home in a more walkable, urban area now that her kids were grown. She wanted a house that was close to town and provided plenty of options for outdoor exercise. An avid follower of real estate, Courtney had always thought of purchasing in St. Augustine and when she came across the listing for the Live Oak House, she immediately scheduled an appointment to view it.

When she visited the house, she fell in love with the architecture, design, and location. She also liked the furnishings that were staged by the architect and interior designer. After a couple of weeks of deliberating, Courtney purchased the home, including all the furnishings. She was attracted to its unique and environmentally sustainable qualities. "Although a lot smaller than my previous house," Courtney says, "the Live Oak House makes a huge statement in terms of its environmental footprint on St. Augustine."

Built to spec by architect Rory Reynolds, the house gets its name from the decades-old live oak tree, a dramatic feature in the main courtyard. The house was specifically designed to preserve the tree and incorporate it into the design. In addition, all of the three levels have outside space, with beautiful views of the 75-year-old tree, the historic St. Augustine Lighthouse, the Intracoastal Waterway (Salt Run), and the Atlantic Ocean.

BUILT TO BE ENERGY EFFICIENT

The house's foundation sits atop a coquina (soft limestone) site, which is a naturally porous soil that allows all of the rainwater to be absorbed back into the aquifer. To create a house as efficient as possible, the Live Oak House was built with double-glazed/impact windows and doors, foam-insulated walls and roof, ENERGY STAR appliances, a smart HVAC system, and an energy recovery ventilator (ERV) to introduce and treat the incoming outdoor air. More than 50% of the windows are located on the north and south façade, taking advantage of passive lighting. Water-Sense fixtures allow the house to use about 35% less water than the average household. With all of these green features, the home's HERS rating at 50 (see the sidebar on p. 149) is estimated to make it twice as efficient as a standard home.

A major challenge for Reynolds was to build this home to high standards while keeping costs in line with typical new construction. Completed at the cost of a standard home, the Live Oak House is the first LEED for Homes Platinum Certification in St. Augustine and was awarded Green Home of the Year by the U.S. Green Building Council's Northeast Florida chapter.

The exterior of the house is clad in stark white stucco and fiber cement lap siding. Fencing was constructed with pressure-treated boards, surrounded by drought-tolerant foliage, which means there's no grass to water.

Additional green features that contributed to LEED certification include building in a walkable neighborhood, preserving 8 of the 11 trees on the property, reducing the overall irrigation demand, using drought-tolerant landscaping, and recycling almost all of the construction waste, with only about 1% going to the landfill. Asked why he built the house small, Reynolds says, "I designed the home to be in perfect harmony with the site. Small was a byproduct of what I considered to be the best design."

And how does Courtney feel? She likes living in a smaller space, with "less to worry about and less mess." She also likes living in a walkable community and hopes that other builders in the area will follow suit and design and build living spaces that work in tandem with the local community.

TOP: The kitchen and dining areas have solid maple cabinetry and a simple design that creates a clean, modern look. Countertops are white concrete.

ABOVE: Rapidly renewable stranded bamboo floors were installed throughout the house.

ABOVE: The master bedroom, located on the second floor and angled away from the living spaces in its own wing, has a private balcony overlooking the oak tree. Lighted shelves under the clerestory windows are designed to bounce light into the home.

RIGHT: The house was built to incorporate interior and exterior spaces with outdoor sitting areas on each level; shown here is the balcony outside the master bedroom.

HERS RATING

The Home Energy Rating System (HERS) is a national standard for energy efficiency developed by RESNET (Residential Energy Services Network), a not-for-profit association. HERS rates the efficiency of a home compared to a standard house with the same dimensions and climate. The Live Oak House has a HERS rating of 50, which indicates that it is 50% more energy efficient than a standard new home at 100. (A home with a HERS Index score of 140 is 40% less energy efficient than a standard new home.) A certified rating provider, working under the supervision of RESNET, determines the individual house rating, which is often used in determining eligibility for programs such as ENERGY STAR. Many older homes have a HERS rating over 100, but many new homes are being built more efficiently and are well under 100. For additional information about this rating, check the website: resnet.us.

GUEST BEDROOM

GUEST BEDROOM

DECK

GARAGE

FIRST FLOOR

LIVING ROOM

KITCHEN/ DINING ROOM

MASTER BEDROOM

SECOND FLOOR

THIRD FLOOR

DOWNSIZING FEATURES
- Low-maintenance materials
- High ceilings
- Lots of windows
- Multiple outdoor spaces
- Walkable community

GREEN FEATURES
- Passive solar lighting
- LED lights
- Energy recovery ventilator (ERV)
- Low-VOC paints, adhesives, and sealants
- Multiple exhaust fans
- WaterSense fixtures (toilets, faucets, and showers)
- Native landscaping
- Permeable lot
- Preservation of trees on the property
- Locally sourced materials
- Green-roof ready
- HERS index: 50 (see the sidebar on p. 149)

The house was designed in a U-shape to preserve the 75-year-old oak tree in the center, creating a courtyard and providing necessary shade. A raised foundation on the northern part of the house protects the tree's roots.

445

ABOVE: The porch, constructed of pressure-treated deck boards, and the custom mahogany front door create a vibrant contrast to the stark white stucco exterior walls.

LEFT: The view from the rear of the house is toward the Salt Run Intracoastal Waterway.

CASCADE MOUNTAIN HOUSE

CONSTRUCTION TYPE:
Timber Frame/SIPs

ARCHITECT:
FabCab

PHOTOGRAPHER:
Dale Lang

LOCATION:
Cle Elum, Wash.

SIZE:
1,527 sq. ft.

SEVERAL YEARS AGO AS BARB AND DAN MATLOCK were approaching retirement, they realized that they didn't want to continue living in Seattle but would rather relocate to a smaller, more rural community, similar to the one they had both grown up in. They decided Cle Elum, in the heart of the Cascade Mountains, would be a good fit with its proximity to the interstate and within an hour and a half drive to Seattle. After several months of searching they found the perfect six-acre lot with wonderful views of the mountains.

In Seattle, they had been living in a large 3,800-sq.-ft. home that required a good deal of maintenance. For their retirement, they didn't want to spend weekends working on the house. Rather they preferred to spend time on their hobbies and interests such as hiking, biking, fly fishing, and quilting. Barb also wanted a place where friends and family could visit and enjoy the Northwest with them. They realized they could have a house with less square footage than their previous home that would meet all of their requirements as long as it was designed efficiently.

THE GREAT PURGE

Moving from 3,800 sq. ft. to 1,500 sq. ft. meant getting rid of a lot of "old baggage." During their 40 years of marriage they had lived in three different homes, each successively larger than the one before. They'd never had to get rid of any belongings and continued to accumulate lots of stuff. In their last house, they had three family/living rooms with three sets of couches and associated lounging chairs to fill up the rooms. In designing this new house they wanted a much more efficient layout and less furniture.

Barb began getting rid of things almost a year before they moved. "Need" was considered over "want." She spent many weekends going through boxes, looking up information (such as how many years of tax returns you need to keep), and organizing their children's yearbooks and other memorabilia. She divided possessions into three categories: "take," which went in the need pile, "sell," and "give away" (to family/friends or charity). It was a lesson in prioritizing and figuring out what she really needed. For example, Barb and Dan sold their piano, which no one played, and donated all the paperback books to Goodwill. They got rid of most of their furniture and all the lawn and landscaping equipment since the new house has no lawn.

Moving was a lot of work, says the couple, but it was nice to get rid of all the clutter accumulated over 40 years. Barb and Dan also considered another advantage of the purge—"not leaving the kids a big mess to figure out once it all gets dropped in their lap."

Minimal windows on the front of the house provide privacy and cut back on heat loss. The siding combines cedar, treated with a clear fire-retardant coating, with corrugated aluminum and a small amount of fiber cement board.

STRUCTURAL INSULATED PANELS (SIPS)

Structural insulated panels (SIPS) are manufactured by sandwiching foam insulation between two outer structural panels (usually oriented strand board or plywood, or even metal). SIPs can be custom designed for a particular house in dimensions as big as 8 ft. x 24 ft. (by comparison, standard plywood sheets are 4 ft. x 8 ft.). SIPs are increasingly popular for building walls, roofs, floors, and even foundations because of their excellent insulating qualities, strength, short construction time, and low waste. In a house built using SIPs, the heating, ventilation, and air conditioning (HVAC) equipment is scaled down to save money, while the house stays comfortable with lower energy costs. To learn more, visit sips.org.

TOP: Although the kitchen is a small space, it is very efficiently designed. The large island is used for food preparation and also as a gathering place when friends come over. A small pantry was added on the side of the kitchen to provide extra storage.

ABOVE: The flex room serves as an office area/den and media room. A sleep sofa (not visible here) allows more room for company.

A barn door to the right and pocket door to the left both present a clean modern look and save space. Native art, by a local artist, enhances the dining area.

MAXIMIZING SPACE WITH POCKET DOORS

Pocket doors are an excellent way to save space, particularly in a small house where swinging doors take up much-needed room. The doors slide, usually on an upper track, and disappear into a pocket inside the adjoining wall. When the pocket door is open, it allows two spaces to be combined, offering flexibility in the use of space and also privacy as desired. Pocket doors also offer a clean aesthetic and can be used with any design style.

A private porch is accessed from the master bedroom. A ceiling fan can be used to help the room feel cool on hot days.

DOWNSIZING FEATURES
- One-floor living
- Barrier-free shower
- Open floor plan
- Vaulted ceilings
- Flexible spaces
- Ample daylighting
- Barn doors
- Pocket doors
- Creative storage
- Large outdoor space

GREEN FEATURES
- Standing-seam metal roof
- Solar panels
- Structural insulated panels (SIPS)
- Natural materials
- Backup power generator
- Ceiling fans
- Detached garage

The main house is heated with a radiant-floor heating system, which the owners set to about 64°F in winter. They use the woodstove for maintaining comfortable temperatures above this level in the kitchen and main living areas. With the abundance of surrounding woods, there is always a good supply of wood for the stove.

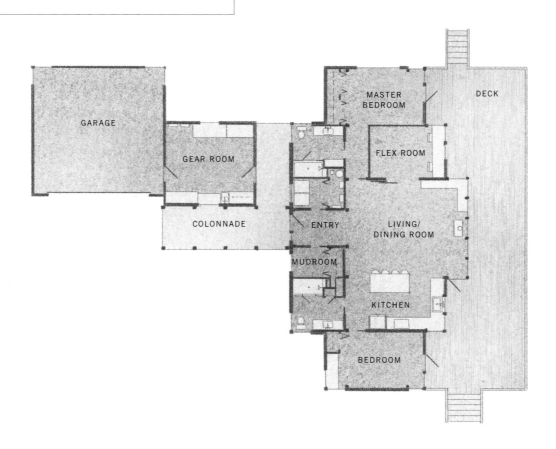

WORKING WITH FABCAB

When the couple began working with the architectural firm FabCab, they were clear about their requirements: a large span of windows to capture the magnificent views, highly energy-efficient construction, natural materials, an open-concept design, a strong connection to the outdoors for all seasons, solar power, lots of storage, an accessible route from the garage to the house, and predictable pricing.

While the interior of the house is considerably smaller, the large deck expands the space and makes the house feel much roomier, as well as providing beautiful views of the mountains. All of the main rooms look out onto the deck and the mountains. A small (350-sq.-ft.) activities room lies across a breezeway, used for some storage but also as a quilting area for Barb and fly-tying bench for Dan.

Since this was to be Barb and Dan's retirement home, FabCab designed it to be viable for aging in place. With an open floor plan and one-floor living, the house has easy access to get around with limited steps. Even the shower is rimless, making it safer to get in and out of.

In order to meet the couple's needs for an energy-efficient house, solar panels were installed on the roof. Structural insulated panels (SIPs) were used to provide high insulation for the enclosure, and a ventilation system was installed as well as a backup generator. Large windows provide ample daylighting to limit the need for electrical lighting.

The great bank of windows on the north side of the house provides an abundance of natural light and breathtaking views of the Cascade Mountains from all the main living areas and the large deck. In addition, the high ceilings make the house feel larger than it is.

WILDFIRE PROTECTION

According to architect Bruce Waltar, the risk of wildfire at this site was an important design criterion. The county requires that all new houses in Wildland-Urban Interface zones (which this is) meet CalFire standards. FabCab's building system has an advantage over stick-built construction in that the SIP roof assembly does not employ attic space that needs to be vented (a common path for embers to ignite a building). The standard required that they enclose the underside of the deck with metal mesh (preventing embers from landing on the underside of the deck framing, another common point of ignition). Other fire-preventive aspects were also incorporated, including the standing-seam metal roof, which is noncombustible, and the metal siding and fiber cement boards, which are fire resistant. For aesthetic reasons, Barb and Dan wished to

FACING PAGE: The back of the house has floor-to-ceiling windows to provide views of the beautiful Cascade Mountains (and the narrow cable railings around the deck do not impede the view). The timber frame is structural and can be seen protruding below the roof.

ABOVE: The colonnade leads to the front entrance and connects with the covered breezeway that provides access to the storage room and garage.

LEFT: As the weather permits, Barb and Dan use the deck daily, eating, entertaining, and enjoying the gas fire and watching the evening stars. They set up several bird feeders off the front of the deck and love to watch the hummingbirds, finches, woodpeckers, and jays that are seasonal visitors.

have some cedar siding, so it was treated with a clear fire-retardant coating.

The couple really loves the feel of the house and its setting. At night they can turn off all the lights and look over the Yakima Valley and mountains that lie to the north and not see another house or light. "It feels like we're 50 miles from civilization even though we're only 3 miles from I-90 and 15 minutes from town."

CONTEMPORARY FARMHOUSE

CONSTRUCTION TYPE:
Panelized

ARCHITECT/BUILDER:
Unity Homes

PHOTOGRAPHER:
James R. Salomon
Photography (unless
otherwise noted)

LOCATION:
Easton, Conn.

SIZE:
1,996 sq. ft.

AMY AND T.J. HANSON WERE LIVING IN A 3,000-SQ.-FT. house in Rye, N.Y., on a tiny lot in close proximity to their neighbors in a town with very high taxes. The house worked fine for them when they were raising their children, but as empty nesters, it no longer served their needs. They wanted a smaller house with much more land in the country.

FINDING A LOT IN THE COUNTRY

They chose to relocate to the town of Easton, Conn., because it was close to both their jobs and they liked its rural feeling. Once they'd made that decision, they drove around looking for land to build on. The lot they ultimately selected had undeveloped land on both sides, which suited them perfectly. It was flat and had already been cleared. A bonus for T.J. was its proximity to a golf course.

After finding the perfect spot to build they were presented with some challenges. Building was a new experience for them and that was daunting. They were in a new town, and they had to find the right people to prep the site. Amy's sister came across Unity Homes on an Internet search, and the couple was impressed with Unity's track record of creating high-performance, low-energy panelized homes that are healthy, comfortable, and durable. Once they'd chosen Unity as the builder, Amy and T.J. then had to go through the red tape of getting permits.

And one final challenge, of course, was disposing of much of the stuff they'd accumulated in their 22 years of living in the Rye house. The couple prepared for downsizing by giving away items like excess kitchen equipment, lamps, blankets, extra bedding, decorative tchotchkes, sports gear, many books, and a pool table. Fortunately, Amy and T.J. were able to take many of their furnishings with them, and they only had to buy a few new pieces for the new house.

MUST-HAVES IN THE NEW HOUSE

Because the couple wanted this to be their forever home, a first-floor bedroom was a requirement. They also wanted an open floor plan and space on the second floor so their adult children could have some privacy when they come back to visit.

Amy and T.J. knew they didn't want to be bogged down with lots of maintenance: they wanted time to enjoy their new home and engage in leisure activities. The house was built with fiber cement siding and a standing-seam roof, both of which require minimal maintenance.

Another must-have was energy efficiency, both for comfort and to save on utility bills. High-efficiency triple-glazed windows are both low

Amy and T.J. wanted the Contemporary Farmhouse to require as little maintenance as possible. With this as a given, the house was built with a standing-seam metal roof, fiber cement siding, and rot-resistant windows made of a strong, durable polymer. The building is also highly energy efficient, with triple-glazed windows and solar panels on the roof, which produce much of the energy required for the house.

Photo courtesy of T.J. Hanson

The predominantly white kitchen is classic farmhouse style, but with some more contemporary touches—such as the stained concrete floor, which functions well as thermal mass and adds to the energy efficiency of the house.

maintenance and rated high for thermal performance and air tightness. Dense-packed cellulose insulation was used in the walls and loose-fill in the roof, creating an excellent R-value in the envelope of the house. An on-demand water heater and air source heat pump both save on energy. In order to keep the interior air healthy with the airtight envelope (0.60 @ ACH50 air tightness), an energy recovery ventilation (ERV) system was built in to exchange the stale interior air with the cleaner outside air.

Amy loves the farmhouse look of the house, with its clean lines and simple forms. The home's roof pitch and massing are reminiscent of other farmhouses in the area. The exterior finishes represent a contemporary take on the board-and-batten siding that is found on many local barns. The generous front porch is a welcoming reminder of the warmth of farmhouse living. And the large meadow that spreads out in front of the house is filled with wildflowers throughout the summer. Amy remarks that ". . . it feels like I'm getting 'away' every time I come home."

CEILING FANS

Ceiling fans move air, which, in turn, carries heat away from the body, driving down body temperature. Fans run counterclockwise in the warm summer. Most fans can run in reverse in the winter, producing an updraft, forcing warm air near the ceiling down to where people are sitting. Ceiling fans can lower air-conditioning and heating costs. They now come in as many styles as any other fixture in the house. Ceiling fans also have a variety of speeds, blade pitch, and controls, and some come with remote controls.

If nobody's in the room, nobody's being cooled off, so fans churning in an empty room just waste electricity. Ceiling fans with light kits that are ENERGY STAR–rated are about 40% more efficient than conventional fan/light units, saving on energy costs and reducing greenhouse gas emissions. The ceiling fan on the porch of the Contemporary Farmhouse is from Emerson (emerson.com).

The covered porch has a blue ceiling, which is a southern tradition variously reputed to scare away evil spirits, repel insects, or bring good luck. The Port Orford cedar used for the decking is hard, strong, and insect and rot resistant. The ceiling fan helps move air around to offer a cooler outdoor experience.

DOWNSIZING FEATURES
- First-floor master bedroom
- Multiple outdoor spaces
- Low-maintenance materials
- Vaulted ceiling

GREEN FEATURES
- High-efficiency windows
- On-demand water heater
- Energy recovery ventilator (ERV)
- Superinsulation
- Concrete floors

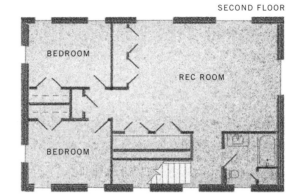

BEDROOM

REC ROOM

BEDROOM

DECK

FIRST FLOOR

KITCHEN

DINING ROOM

LIVING ROOM

MASTER BEDROOM

ENTRY

PORCH

The large meadow in front of the house is filled with wildflowers, helping to make this permanent residence feel like a vacation home.

LEFT: The high vaulted ceiling in the living room, finished with whitewashed pine boards, complements the whitewashed structural timbers visible in the kitchen/dining areas and creates a more expansive feel. The large triple-glazed tilt-and-turn windows allow for natural ventilation and lots of daylighting, along with ease of cleaning.

BELOW: The panels for the house were manufactured in Keane, N.H., in the Unity Homes Production Facility equipped with computer numerical control (CNC) machines controlled by information from the 3D computer model of the house. These machines produce parts that are extremely precise.
Photo courtesy of Heather Holloway

CITY HOUSE ON THE RIVER

CONSTRUCTION TYPE:
Site Built

ARCHITECT:
Anik Péloquin, Anik
Péloquin Architecte

PHOTOGRAPHER:
Alberto Biscaro

LOCATION:
Montreal, Quebec,
Canada

SIZE:
1,360 sq. ft.

FOR 15 YEARS, MARIANGELA LIVED IN A HOUSE IN the north end of Montreal. The house was typical of the brick bungalows of the 1950s, with tiny windows, three small rooms upstairs, a kitchen on the ground floor that everyone had to pass through to get to the other rooms, and a large basement, undefined except for a small laundry area. The redeeming quality of the house was the wonderful 5,000-sq.-ft. garden at the rear of the property, but the openings from the house to the garden were limited.

After she'd lived in the house for about a year, Mariangela worked with architect Anik Péloquin to redefine the space by adding onto the main house and opening it up to the large garden. With the addition, the 2,000-sq.-ft. house grew to 2,600 sq. ft. and completely changed Mariangela's experience being inside and outside the house, with much more flexibility and accessibility to the garden. As she says, "it was a joy to live in the house for 15 years."

FINDING A NEW HOME

As she approached retirement, Mariangela began to reflect on where she wanted to live and what was important for the future. In her own words, she longed for "simplicity, leisure, serenity, calm, and travel." She also harbored a secret desire to have a riverfront home in the city. As such, she was excited when she found a summerhouse for sale on a 48-ft.-wide parcel of land, in front of the Des Prairies River close to town. She decided to buy it and tear down the house to build one that was more to her style. Building a new house on that property however was a challenge. With setbacks of 18 ft., there was only 30 ft. left for the house (most people build far bigger houses on the riverside of this street on lots that are larger). In order to stay within her construction budget, Mariangela chose to build the house small and invest in quality materials rather than more square footage. With retirement looming, she sought an intimate space with limited maintenance requirements.

DOWNSIZING WAS A PROCESS

For Mariangela, the downsizing process began when she was living in her previous house. In an effort to simplify her living conditions, she'd started to get rid of unnecessary items and to choose which ones she really needed.

She also looked at the house she was living in to see which areas were of little or no use so she could plan better for her future home. She added up all the areas of the house that went unused: her sewing area

FACING PAGE: Privacy is always an issue on a busy street, so the architect used few windows on the front of the house. The entry door is recessed to break up the flat façade, and wood siding mixed in with the brick adds interest to the exterior. Plantings are all indigenous and require minimal care.

that she'd rarely used in her 15 years there; her guest room that was never occupied; and her living room, which served as a showplace rather than a living area. This exercise done, she decided that her future home would not be for show, and instead all the spaces would have a purpose.

Mariangela had no trouble getting rid of plenty of household items. She started with the large furniture (couches and chests of drawers), which she gave to her friend's daughter. Then she got rid of the smaller knickknacks and trinkets. She donated her books to a feminist organization, and many items went to Goodwill. Some of the furnishings she took to her new house and repurposed them for other uses, such as the sideboard, which became a bookshelf.

RIGHT AND BELOW: The first floor plan is open, with a single floor-to-ceiling partition separating the living room from the dining room and kitchen. Sliding panels along the unit can be left open or closed for privacy or just to hide dirty dishes from company.

The upstairs bathroom is all tile, which requires minimal maintenance. Kaleidoscope-colored glass mosaic tiles on one wall and a vanity in orange laminate provide a nice contrast with the otherwise all-white bathroom.

ADJUSTING TO A SMALLER SPACE

It helped that Mariangela had experience working with Anik on the addition to her previous house. When she began this project, she told Anik that she wanted an affordable house that was cozy, modern, light filled with full-length windows, and low maintenance, with a focus on the river and garden just outside the house. And Anik delivered.

The new house is just about half the size of her previous one, but there is an abundance of light and the soothing sound of the running waters of the river. She has been careful to decorate with more neutral colors and use well-chosen objects so as not to disrupt the beautiful scenery surrounding the house. And because the house is so minimalistic, it substantially reduces the amount of maintenance required.

FIRST FLOOR

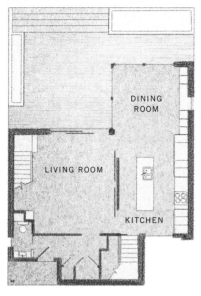

DINING ROOM

LIVING ROOM

KITCHEN

SECOND FLOOR

BEDROOM

OPEN TO BELOW

BEDROOM

DOWNSIZING FEATURES
• Double-height ceilings
• Large windows
• Large patio

GREEN FEATURES
• Native plantings
• Permeable paving
• LED lighting
• Local materials

ABOVE: Access to the second floor is by way of a minimal steel staircase with open risers, which allows light and air to flow though.

FACING PAGE: In contrast to the buttoned-up front façade, the rear of the house opens up with a wall of windows and views to the river. Easy access to the patio through sliding doors on the living room and dining room extends the feeling of space in the house. The exterior is a combination of brick and thermally modified ("roasted") wood.

"ROASTED" OR THERMALLY MODIFIED WOOD

Roasting wood is a method of treating wood by putting it in a vacuum-regulated kiln at very high temperatures. In the kiln oxygen is removed, causing the wood to roast. The resulting color is uniformly dark and consistent throughout. This process creates a wood that is very stable, decay- and moisture-resistant, chemical-free, and with a surface at a lower risk of mold.

Thermally modified wood was an ideal material to use on the house near the water since this method reduces shrinkage, bending, and swelling and creates a wood that is resistant to humidity and temperature changes.

PASSIVE DACHA

CONSTRUCTION TYPE:
Site Built

**ARCHITECT/GENERAL
CONTRACTOR:**
Timothy Lock, GO Logic

PHOTOGRAPHER:
Josh Gerritsen Media

LOCATION:
Monroe, Maine

SIZE:
1,000 sq. ft.

ALISON RECTOR HAS AN INTERESTING THEORY ON downsizing: "Why drive a five-person vehicle when you're mostly driving one or two people? I feel the same way about the square footage of home and downsizing." She and her husband, Eric, were ready to downsize, and for their new home they wanted a smaller environmental footprint and near zero operational costs. They subdivided the 100 acres that they owned, sold their home and barn on the 20-acre property, and on the remaining 80 acres (most of it woods) built themselves a smaller house just about a quarter of a mile away.

The house they'd lived in for the previous 21 years was 2,800 sq. ft. They were accustomed to losing power for short periods of time over the years, but when an ice storm in 1998 knocked out power for about 11 days, they began to find solutions to their energy issues. Over the next several months they installed a few solar panels, a battery, an inverter, and some simple lights on the advice of architect Alan Gibson, who later partnered with Matthew O'Malia to form GO Logic. Making these alterations to their farmhouse was a great experience for the Rectors in preparing them to build an almost totally off-the-grid house in the future.

Alison and Eric chose GO Logic to design/build their new home because of their past experience with Alan and the firm's leadership in quantifiable energy-efficient design/build and Passive House standards. Although their house is fully functional without grid power, they chose to be connected to the grid, sending excess power to the grid when they don't need it and getting power when they do.

HEATING AND COOLING THE HOUSE

The heat in the Passive Dacha is primarily generated by the big triple-glazed southern windows and stored by the insulated concrete slab flooring. It is supplemented by a propane space heater that requires only a little electricity to run the controls and the fan. In the past winter, Alison and Eric used just 47 gallons of propane that cost them $128 and reportedly kept them "toasty warm." An on-demand hot-water heater provides the hot water required and uses minimal electricity to power its controls. All of the lights in the Dacha are LED, most of them powered by a 12v circuit that comes directly off the battery bank.

The insulated concrete slab—their foundation and flooring—plays an integral part in the passive heating system. As thermal mass, it stores heat from the sun in the winter, and in the summer, when the sun's angle is higher and the sun's rays are blocked from the interior, the slab maintains an even temperature inside the house.

This highly efficient home is a modern interpretation of a rural retreat (*dacha* in Russian) with the functionality of a Passive House. The roof of the garage houses a photovoltaic (PV) array charging an interior battery pack, which allows the house to be net zero and partially off-the-grid.

Even though the kitchen is smaller in terms of square footage, it is much more functional than the couple's previous kitchen, so it feels bigger. All of the appliances are under counter, allowing for ample counter workspace.

THE PROCESS OF DOWNSIZING

The Rectors were both shocked at how much they had packed away inside the farmhouse and barn during the 21 years they lived there. "One goal in moving was to create an efficient house and another was to accomplish the downsizing that we knew we wanted to do," Eric says. Cutting their square footage in half meant disposing of at least half of their possessions. Once they sold their home and began the process of building their new one, they spent a few days a month over 18 months, sorting through items and deciding what should be sold and what should be given away. They also needed to move the contents of Alison's in-town art studio to her new one, which was integrated within the garage building of the new house. Because there were so many moving parts to this process, it felt like a sprint to the finish line when the new owners were close to moving into the farmhouse.

Once all the boxes were settled into their new home, Alison and Eric realized they weren't done purging, because there was no way it would all fit. They transferred all the boxes to Alison's office and proceeded to go about their second selection and purging process over the next six months until they had finally reached a balance of having adequate living space while maintaining some of their important possessions. That second purge was the most difficult part of the move.

Dry-finished white oak cabinetry inspired by mid-20th-century mini-malist art and furniture in the living room holds many of the books and other items that survived their several purges. The double-height kitchen/dining/living space gives the home an airier feel than the square footage would suggest.

ADA-COMPLIANT DOORS

Congress passed the Americans with Disabilities Act (ADA) in 1990. It was the first comprehensive civil rights law protecting the needs of people with disabilities. One part of this act ensures access to the built environment for people with disabilities by establishing design requirements for the construction and alteration of facilities subject to the law. Although the act does not mandate homes to comply with these standards, some people opt to comply with some of them so they'll be able to age in place comfortably. The standards for door openings require a minimum width of 32 in. and a maximum width of 48 in. The measurement is taken between the face of the door and the stop of the frame with the door open to 90 degrees. Alison and Eric opted to build their home using these door standards so they could prepare for any future needs.

LIVING IN A SMALLER SPACE

Even though it was a difficult process, Eric and Alison say they are delighted, relieved of burden, and feel socially more responsible living in their smaller house. They appreciate that their living space is actually more than most people in the world can afford and are grateful for the well-

All of the materials used for the house were designed to be maintenance free, including the standing-seam metal roof and COR-TEN steel siding. The garage is clad in horizontal shiplap white cedar siding. Clerestory windows along the front of the garage/studio/sleeping loft allow a lot of light while also providing privacy.

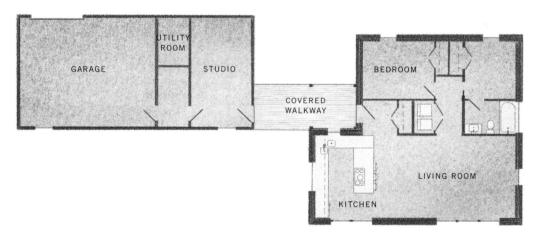

DOWNSIZING FEATURES
• One-floor living
• Grab bars in shower
• Maintenance-free materials/design
• ADA-compliant doors
• Minimal steps at entrances
• Flex space

GREEN FEATURES
• Passive House (PH) standard design (uncertified)

• Photovoltaic (PV) panels
• Heat recovery ventilator (HRV)
• Low-voltage electrical delivery
• Smart temperature control system
• Superinsulation
• Triple-glazed windows
• ENERGY STAR appliances
• LED lights
• Concrete floors
• Detached garage

designed 1,000-sq.-ft. space they have. They don't miss the larger space they had been using for the past 21 years: Even when they hosted a party for 25 people in their new home, "it never felt cramped."

Downsizing was one of the best choices Alison and Eric have ever made. In addition to their comfort, the savings in energy make Passive House a very efficient method of building. Alison is delighted that it takes her just 15 minutes to vacuum the whole house. "The house is low maintenance and self-sufficient; we can leave the house for extended periods of time, even in winter, without concern that pipes are going to freeze," she says.

Eric is very satisfied being able to limit their resource needs to a tiny fraction of what they used in the past while maintaining or even increasing the comfort of their daily lives. He further believes that all of the technology used to achieve this cozy net-zero home is affordable to the average American; his is not a one-off experiment. "This is truly a proof of concept and could become the future of home construction."

ABOVE AND LEFT: A walkway separates the main house from the garage/studio, with a covered entranceway and bench providing the perfect place to remove wet boots or just enjoy the outdoors. Alison's studio is in this garage building, with a sleeping loft above. Because the couple both work at home, it is much easier when there is an option to physically separate at times in order to focus, listen to music, or talk on the phone.

MONTROSE PLACE BUNGALOW

CONSTRUCTION TYPE:
Remodel

ARCHITECT:
David Heide Design
Studio

PHOTOGRAPHER:
Greg Page Photography
(unless otherwise noted)

LOCATION:
St. Paul, Minn.

SIZE:
2,000 sq. ft.

THE LONGER THEY LIVED IN THEIR 3,800-SQ.-FT. house in Eagan, a suburb about eight miles south of St. Paul, Minn., the more Sandy and Tim began to feel that maintenance of the house and yard was more than they wanted to handle. So after raising their children in the suburbs, they decided to move back to the city and downsize to a classic 1922 bungalow. The couple selected this house because they say it "had good bones." They also liked its proximity to the Mississippi River, a local college campus, and great walking and biking opportunities.

The small, but attractive house they found in St. Paul had been stripped of its millwork, built-ins, and much of its Arts and Crafts charm during the 1950s. Architect David Heide made it his mission to put the charm back into the bungalow while creating the open living spaces desired for the couple's more modern way of life. The challenge was to create these open spaces in a vintage house without compromising its historic structure.

LIVING SMALLER
It took Sandy and Tim a good three rounds of purges to downsize from their former home. There were certain items of furniture they were hoping to fit into their new home, such as a lovely Arts and Crafts bench seat, but they realized they would take up too much room. They gradually became more and more ruthless as the time came closer to having to move out of one house and into the other.

Within two years of moving, Sandy and Tim both retired. It was admittedly an adjustment for them to be sharing the same space, which was smaller than what they'd been used to. In time, however, they got used to being together for most of the day—and they're happy that cursory housecleaning now takes only a half hour.

Although they don't miss the larger house, they do miss the beautiful space that it looked out on. They have had to adjust to living in an urban environment, with homes close to them on both sides and the sounds that necessarily come with it: dogs barking, radios playing, neighborhood construction projects, and so on. On the positive side, they enjoy the sounds of the bagpiper who lives a few blocks away as well as the soft sounds of a beginner cellist from across the alley.

BRINGING BACK ARTS AND CRAFTS STYLE
Sandy and Tim have always liked the Arts and Crafts style and had tried to incorporate it into the decor of their previous house. With this renovation they had the opportunity to bring back the old 1922 bungalow style and

The exterior of the house was resurfaced with acrylic stucco (the cement stucco of the original house [inset] was cracked and deteriorating), and much of the exterior millwork was replaced with fiber cement siding for durability.
Photo by Michael Crull of DHD Studio; inset photo by Mark Nelson of DHD Studio

get the modern amenities that they desired, such as a cook's kitchen and more bathrooms.

Unfortunately, the house had been indifferently remodeled over the years with much of its bungalow character altered or lost. The living spaces had been transformed to remove the separation and definition of spaces that is characteristic of the bungalow style. The architect designed a layout that brought back the Arts and Crafts style but accommodated today's lifestyle. Although the floor plan is still open, definition between rooms was created with period-correct woodwork. Since

Bungalows of the period typically had large cased openings between the living and dining rooms. The architect used this same idea to create a layering of spaces connecting the living room, dining room, side entry, and kitchen.

the couple expressed a desire to grow old in the house, accessibility issues were also addressed in the design, such as installing a barrier-free shower.

During the remodel, the house was stripped to the bones and rebuilt to include new energy-efficient windows and doors, spray foam insulation, and energy-efficient mechanical and electrical systems. In the process, the entire floor plan was rearranged to bring the house back to its original-era style and to make it more accessible. Appropriate period cabinetry and architectural details, such as reproduction lighting and tile, were added, much of it designed by the architect. And replacing windows with larger ones improved daylighting and the house's connection to the landscape.

Sandy and Tim were looking for a house that could be their forever home and that is what they achieved. Having the new master suite on the main floor allows them to feel secure that they can comfortably grow old in this house. And it is close to family and is more manageable in terms of maintenance. "We always feel good about walking through the door after a vacation or time away.

And as the last few years have allowed our landscaping to mature, our backyard has become a wonderful sanctuary."

DAYLIGHTING

Daylighting is the practice of lighting an interior space using natural light rather than electric light. This technique is particularly important in a small house because it creates a more open and spacious feel. Natural light is usually more pleasing, reduces electrical use and the heat created by artificial lighting, and connects the indoors with the outdoors. And if that isn't enough, studies show that the use of daylighting in schools and offices increases productivity. Excellent daylighting can be achieved when the orientation of the house takes optimal advantage of the sun and all the windows are arranged to grab as much daylight as possible.

KITCHEN

PORCH

BACK ENTRY

MASTER BEDROOM

DINING ROOM

LIVING ROOM

FIRST FLOOR

ENTRY PORCH

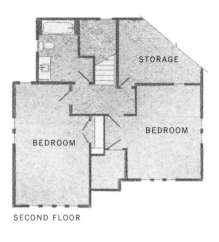

STORAGE

BEDROOM

BEDROOM

SECOND FLOOR

DOWNSIZING FEATURES
• Main-floor master bedroom
• Open floor plan
• Daylighting
• Barrier-free shower

GREEN FEATURES
• Old house remodeling
• Reused materials
• Spray foam insulation
• Highly efficient windows and doors
• Energy-efficient HVAC
• Work by local artisans

Bathroom tile and reproduction lights were selected for their period-appropriate design.

ABOVE AND LEFT: A small patio on the side of the house provides a comfortable sitting area for relaxing or dining, while a paved walkway leads to another sitting area out back.

ENABLE BY NORTHWESTERN

CONSTRUCTION TYPE:
Structural Insulated
Panels (SIPs)

ARCHITECT/BUILDER:
Students and Faculty
and Partners of
Northwestern University

PHOTOGRAPHER:
Dennis Schroeder
(unless otherwise
noted); U.S. Department
of Energy Solar
Decathlon

LOCATION:
Solar Decathlon 2017 in
Denver, Colo.

SIZE:
994 sq. ft.

THE SOLAR DECATHLON TEAM AT NORTHWESTERN University was inspired to build Enable by the aging community in Evanston, Illinois., where their school is located. (Enable stands for two of their core beliefs: ENergized, which refers both to energy efficiency and an active lifestyle, and AdaptABLE, meeting residents' changing needs) About 20% of the population in the town is projected to be 65 and older by 2020. However, only 1% of the current housing supply is suitable for this population.

The students did extensive research, interviewing their target population to define the needs and desires of this baby boom generation. In addition, they investigated new and relevant technologies by working with professionals in construction, energy, architecture, and design. Their primary goal was to design and build a house that is beautiful, accessible, comfortable, innovative, energy efficient, and easy to maintain—with "no compromises" in any area.

PROSPECTIVE HOMEOWNERS

The team envisioned an imaginary married couple, Michael and Lisa, who were typical of the demographic they were designing the house for. Michael is 55 and Lisa is 53, and both are at the later end of the baby boom generation. With one of their children in college and the other living with her fiancé in St. Louis, they are recent empty nesters in Evanston, Ill., just north of Chicago. Both Michael and Lisa plan to retire in 10 to 15 years, Michael from his banking firm in Chicago, where he commutes daily, and Lisa from her at-home graphic design work. They are thinking about downsizing now and want a smaller house that is "easy to maintain, comfortable, versatile, durable, and a place they could see themselves living in for the rest of their lives." The house needs to accommodate their active lifestyles while not taking up their free time with lots of maintenance. They want a forever home that will function for them if they need to take care of an elderly parent or if they at some point become less nimble themselves.

In designing their house for baby boomers, the team also built it to meet the accessibility requirements of the Americans with Disabilities Act (ADA). To accomplish this, the team included features that would support the needs of future residents, such as zero-step entrances, single-floor living, wide hallways and doorways, wheelchair-accessible light switches, and lever-style door handles and faucets.

The exterior of the house was designed to be as sustainable and low-maintenance as possible, making it ideal for downsizers. Sustainably forested siding (including thermally modified timber on some elevations) is durable, low-maintenance, and environmentally responsible. A roof-integrated solar panel system (not visible) is another innovation.

A HOUSE OF INNOVATIONS

Solar Decathlon teams are encouraged to use new technologies and not necessarily stay with old methods and off-the-shelf materials. The Enable team selected several innovations for this house particularly suited for boomers.

Prefabricated interior modular walls are easily reconfigured to accommodate occupants' changing needs. Exterior walls were built using prefabricated structural insulated panels (SIPs), which offer optimum energy efficiency, acoustic separation, fast installation, and structural strength. The use of SIPs allowed the team to provide an open living space for ADA access, without structural walls or columns.

Another important new innovation used here is spray coating applied to the interior and exterior surfaces of the windows and other exterior façades. These photocatalytic surfaces self-clean, improve indoor air quality, and cut down on maintenance, all important for aging in place. With this new technology, sunlight activates the coating to break down volatile organic compounds (VOCs) and organic grime on surfaces and keep them clean while purifying the air.

Self-watering planters ("Breathe Walls") in the living room cut down on maintenance while also allowing residents to enjoy natural greenery. An indoor monitoring system reports on air quality, tracking VOCs, CO_2, dust, humidity, and temperature.

The team won top awards at the event, coming in first for Market Potential and Communications by delivering "a message of sustainability without compromise that is consistently articulated in concert with their materials and technology." They are partnering with Berthoud, Colo., Habitat for Humanity to reassemble the Enable house in Colorado as affordable housing.

TOP: Enable's three-season sunroom allows residents to make the most of Chicago's months of warm weather: It is closable during the spring and fall to retain thermal gains and can fully open during the summer to allow for passive ventilation and cooling.

ABOVE: ENERGY STAR appliances keep energy use down. The back panel of the center island is made of the same durable glass that is used for cell phone screens, made by Corning.

Although this house is less than 1,000 sq. ft., it is flexible for entertaining (for example, the dining table expands to seat up to 10 people). The modular wall system allows the space to be reconfigured as required for future needs. The "Breathe Wall" on either side of the opening to the master bedroom is a vertical, living plant self-watering wall system.

Photo courtesy of Josh Bauer/U.S. Department of Energy Solar Decathlon

The second bedroom can be used as an office and/or a bedroom for guests. In the future, it could become a suite for an in-home caregiver, allowing the homeowners to age in place. The sliding door minimizes space otherwise needed for a swinging door, and the handles are large and easy to use for those who are dexterously challenged.

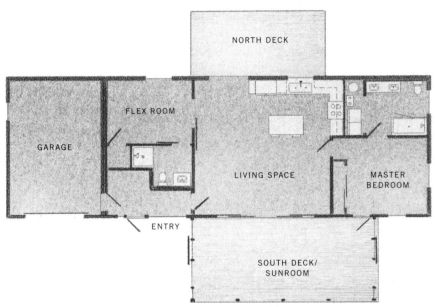

DOWNSIZING FEATURES

- Flexible interior walls for changing needs
- Sunroom for indoor-outdoor living
- Active ventilation for better indoor air quality
- One-floor living
- Wide hallways and doorways
- Barrier-free shower
- Meets ADA accessibility requirements

GREEN FEATURES

- Roof-integrated solar panels
- Energy recovery ventilator (ERV)
- WaterSense fixtures
- ENERGY STAR appliances
- Smart home features
- Indoor house plants to help purify the air
- Air-quality monitoring system
- Self-cleaning treatment on windows and other exterior surfaces
- Sustainably forested siding

The bathroom in the master suite has grab bars and a curbless shower for aging in place. Tile is sustainably manufactured by Crossville, using pre-consumer waste from TOTO toilets.

Photo courtesy of Monika Wnuk/ Northwestern University

SOLAR DECATHLON

Since the first event in 2002, the Solar Decathlon (SD) has generally been held every two years in the United States, initially in Washington, D.C., and more recently in Irvine, Calif., and Denver, Colo. International events have also been held in Spain, China, Dubai, Hungary, Morocco, and Colombia. To compete in the event, thousands of students from universities around the world design and build houses that are efficient at both collecting and converting sunlight into usable energy. Houses are also built using a variety of methods to make them as energy efficient, economical, and healthy as possible. Often techniques are developed that are highly innovative and may be marketed commercially today or in the future. The U.S. Department of Energy

(DOE) sponsors the Solar Decathlon, which is organized by the National Renewable Energy Laboratory.

Visitors tour the houses, where student guides describe the mechanics, systems, and materials while explaining why they chose those options. The contests within the competition vary from event to event in this country and around the world. They focus on current market conditions, feedback from teams and DOE goals in this country, and market conditions and policies internationally for those events. Future SD events are planned in Dubai in 2020 as part of the World Expo and on the National Mall in Washington D.C., where it all began, as part of the Smithsonian Folklife Festival. For further information, visit the Solar Decathlon's website at solardecathlon.gov.

THE JUST RIGHT HOUSE

CONSTRUCTION TYPE:
Site Built

ARCHITECT/BUILDER:
Wolfworks

PHOTOGRAPHER:
Jamie Wolf

LOCATION:
Mansfield, Conn.

SIZE:
1,600 sq. ft.

CERTIFICATIONS:
ENERGY STAR

LIKE MANY OTHER HOMEOWNERS FEATURED IN THIS book, Louise and Paul no longer liked the idea of living in a "too-big" house with unused space that needs to be maintained, heated, and cooled. In their case, they prefer to think of it as "right-sizing" rather than downsizing. After living in a 2,400-sq.-ft. house with unused rooms they were ready for a change. Today, although they have less space, all the space they have gets used. And because the living room, dining room, and kitchen are all connected, the house feels more open.

The couple, both biology professors at the University of Connecticut, liked the idea of being able to walk or ride their bicycles to the campus. Although the house they lived in before was only about five miles away, they say it was a little too far to walk. Now the two-mile distance is easily walkable, with beautiful scenery of a cascading stream down a narrow ravine and around a pond or through a forest. In bad weather, they can skip the last half of the walk by jumping on a campus bus.

PREPARING TO RIGHT-SIZE

Several years before moving, Louise and Paul began the process of clearing out their accumulated possessions. They began by eliminating long-unused lawn tools and other items that had built up in the garage as well as boxes in the basement that hadn't been opened in 20 years! They disposed of a bed in one room to make it an office, and the purge continued.

Because Louise and Paul got rid of so many of their things over time, they didn't have much to do when it came time to move. They advise anyone considering downsizing to try to get rid of things they don't need or use before taking the step of moving into a smaller home. "If you've already effectively downsized before you move," they say, "then you know you will be happy with the end result." Louise and Paul now have just enough storage space to be comfortable, but not enough to encourage them to accumulate things they don't use regularly. Their goal is to have less clutter and enjoy the items they have around them. Because they like living the way they do, they're motivated to keep the process of elimination ongoing.

MUST-HAVES IN THE NEW HOUSE

Louise and Paul knew exactly what they wanted for their new house when they began working with their architect/builder, Jamie Wolf of Wolfworks: a first-floor master suite so that stairs could be avoided in later years; an open floor plan combining kitchen, dining room, and living room into one open space; a large kitchen with plenty of counter space and a gener-

Fiber-cement siding and a durable standing-seam roof keep exterior maintenance to a minimum. The photovoltaic (PV) panels provide 100% of the energy required for the house.

FIRST-FLOOR MASTER BEDROOMS

First-floor master bedrooms are an increasingly popular feature not only in homes for downsizers but in larger houses as well; many people prefer not to have to climb stairs on a regular basis, and some want separation from their children on another floor. First-floor bedrooms are an obvious choice for people who want to age in place. Having the master bedroom on the main floor will avoid the need to use steps when mobility may be compromised, either by age or disability. With the large current baby boomer population, having a first-floor master bedroom is also likely to increase the resale value of the house.

Building a master on the first floor can also serve temporarily as a more private guest room or mother-in-law suite until the time comes when parents want the separation and privacy that the room will provide them. At the time when children move out of the house, the adults may be able to turn down the heat and air conditioning on the second level, minimizing their utility bills as well as saving their knees.

Every little bit of space in this house is well used, including the book niche partway up the stairs.

ous uninterrupted island; a screened porch; and a patio to extend the living space outdoors during the warmer months. They also wanted a guest bedroom, an office/bedroom, two and a half bathrooms, a laundry room, a mudroom, and a green zero-energy design.

In terms of style, the owners favored the look of a typical New England farmhouse. The interconnecting and cascading rooflines, the sheltering porch roof connecting to the garage (or barn in yesteryear), the white exterior, and the general simplicity are all reminiscent of farmhouses from the mid-19th century and turn of the century, when additions were often added on to the original home. Jamie designed the house with two small bedrooms on the second floor. Unlike many garages in new homes today, this house has a one-car garage, reflecting the owners' commitment to walking, biking, and public transportation.

The expansive wall of glass in the dining area floods the house with light. Flooring on the main level is engineered oak.

BUILDING A ZERO-ENERGY HOUSE

Energy efficiency was a priority. Louise and Paul didn't want to worry about future fluctuations in energy availability or prices and were encouraged by the incentives being provided in the state of Connecticut. Their previous house was truly uncomfortable for much of the year. While it was possible for them to keep that house at a comfortable 70°F in winter, it would cost more in propane than they could afford, so they kept it at 62°F and wore lots of sweaters and used comforters.

Louise and Paul sought out Wolfworks as the ideal design/build company because of their vast experience building net-zero homes. And they are delighted with how efficient the new house is. Because the house is so well insulated, they can now comfortably wear a T-shirt and shorts in the house in January, and the windows and doors are no longer cold spots to avoid as they were in the old house. All this costs essentially nothing (except for the cost of connecting to the grid) because the house is net zero; all the heating and cooling it requires is generated by the sun.

ACHIEVING NET ZERO

In addition to designing the house with a good thermal envelope, Wolfworks included several mechanical systems to make the house very efficient and also comfortable and healthy. A heat recovery ventilation (HRV) system was installed that exchanges the interior warm or cool air with exterior fresh air, while maintaining the generated heat or cool. This keeps the house comfortable and healthy—and avoids having allergens and VOCs in the air.

Jamie Wolf says energy security (avoiding fluctuations in energy costs) is important to all his clients in this demographic. In addition, the health, comfort, and durability (low maintenance) that comes with high-performance home practices are all in sync with what people looking to downsize value.

Louise and Paul really like living in a home that has just the right amount of living space. "We do not have to worry about cleaning rooms we never use, and there is no room to accumulate things that we don't need or use on a regular basis. Right-sizing alleviates stresses that you don't even realize you are experiencing!" As a result of the excellent design, the house was awarded the CT Zero Energy Challenge for best thermal envelope in 2018. ·

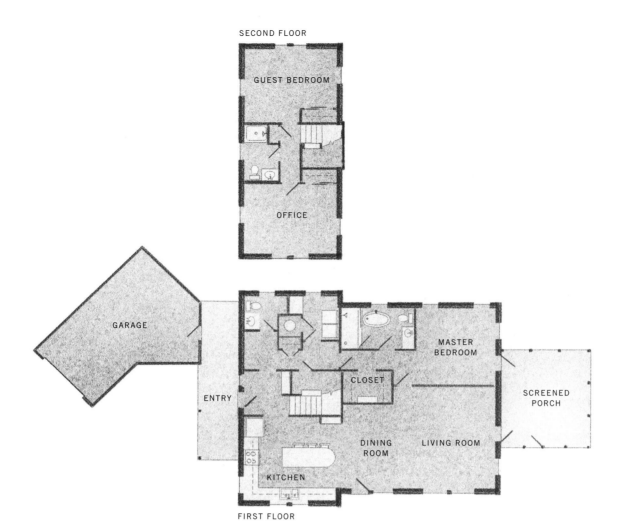

SECOND FLOOR

GUEST BEDROOM

OFFICE

GARAGE

ENTRY

CLOSET

MASTER
BEDROOM

SCREENED
PORCH

DINING
ROOM

LIVING ROOM

KITCHEN

FIRST FLOOR

The rolling barn door creates a wide, easily accessible opening as well as a dramatic entrance to this cozy bathroom with a soaking tub and barrier-free shower.

DOWNSIZING FEATURES
- One-floor living
- Minimal hallways
- Barrier-free shower
- Daylighting
- Spacious outdoor areas

GREEN FEATURES
- Mini-split heat pump
- Heat recovery ventilator (HRV)
- PV panels
- Separate garage
- LED lighting
- Triple-glazed windows
- Heat pump water heater and dryer
- ENERGY STAR appliances
- Optimal solar orientation
- Detached garage

ABOVE LEFT: White base cabinets and open shelving keep the room looking light and airy. Storage is plentiful in the kitchen, and the large quartz island and countertop provide a generous amount of prep space.

ABOVE RIGHT: Triple-glazed tilt-and-turn windows provide excellent natural ventilation and also allow easy access for cleaning.

LEFT: The seasonal screened porch overlooking an adjacent farm serves as a wonderful second patio during the summer. The giant granite boulders that were excavated from the site to build the house were used to create great "sitting rocks" around the outside patio.

NAPA HOUSE

CONSTRUCTION TYPE:
Modular

DESIGNER:
Living Homes

FABRICATOR:
Plant Prefab, Inc.

CONTRACTOR:
Bruce Tucker
Construction

PHOTOGRAPHER:
PlanOmatic

LOCATION:
Napa, Calif.

SIZE:
1,300 sq. ft.

CERTIFICATION:
LEED for Homes
Platinum

AS A CHEF FOR 20 YEARS, CRAIG HAS ALWAYS HAD a respect for the environment, learning to nurture diners by sourcing only the finest quality ingredients, whether organically grown, raised without antibiotics, or free range/cage free. For Craig, it was always about protecting the environment over the whole life cycle of the food. So when he had the chance to develop a property for himself, it was only natural that he would do it in an environmentally responsible way.

MOVING TO A GREENER, DOWNSIZED LIFE

Craig was living in a 2,400-sq.-ft. house in Oakville, Calif., when he came to the realization that he wanted to live a "greener" life and build a home that was resource-efficient and that met his environmental values. His desire to downsize was based on living with only what is needed, a lesson he'd learned after seeing people fill huge homes with stuff that does not fulfill them (and have to maintain, clean, and condition them). That did not align with his values.

As we have seen, for some people, downsizing is extremely stressful but Craig claims that he actually enjoyed the experience. He gave stuff to friends, to Goodwill, and sold some things through eBay. For him, downsizing made him consider what is important and what is not, and his new home has brought him true comfort.

An important criterion for Craig before he began the process of building a new home for himself and his 79-year-old mom was his desire to reduce his carbon footprint and his impact on the environment. Building a house that could be Platinum LEED-certified was very important to him. With this goal in mind, the house was built using recycled building materials (including the wood floors and bathroom tiles) and with no-VOC paint. The ductless, clean-air HVAC system is zoned to heat only the rooms that are being used.

WORKING WITH LIVING HOMES

Craig was extremely thorough in researching the best design companies for green development, and Living Homes rose to the top of his list. He spoke to Steve Glenn, founder and CEO of Living Homes, and after visiting one of his homes, meeting his team, and learning more about the company, Craig decided this was the right firm for him.

It took two and a half years for Craig to finally get his building permit because he first had to install an engineered septic system and a new well. After getting the permit it took only four months from the start of the build to the installation of the modular house on site.

The U-shaped configuration creates privacy for the owner and his guests on both wings of the house (the master bedroom is to the left and the guest room to the right). The fiber cement siding and metal roofing are low-maintenance (and also noncombustible).

Craig wanted a large outdoor lanai where he could entertain and prepare foods using much of what he plans to grow in his garden. The flooring here is graphite-colored sealed concrete scored in 2-ft. squares. Craig liked the industrial look of the steel so chose not to treat it. ("Iron Dog" on the beam is the name of the steel fabricator.) Commercial stainless-steel propane heaters hang from the ceiling for use on cool days and evenings.

In addition to the green features, Craig wanted the ability to customize the design of his new home to truly make it his own. His must-haves included a desire to bring the outdoors in, with a feeling of openness, lots of natural light, a simple design, and quality finishes. Throughout the process, he says, he dreamed about how the design would come together; in the end, it turned out better than he ever imagined.

CHEF'S PLAYGROUND

It's no surprise that Craig loves entertaining and sharing his passion for food. The rear of the house was designed as Craig's culinary center, or as he puts it, his "chef's playground with culinary toys." He wanted an industrial open kitchen space like the professional kitchens he has cooked in. There are plans to install a wood-burning oven in the corner of the cooking wall. The dining room and wet bar are part of the culinary center, all sheltered under the lanai that runs the full width of the back of the house.

Craig's playground was also designed as an area to create culinary provisions from the three-quarter acre culinary gardens he is developing. The house looks out on pinot noir vineyards, and Craig plans to grow over 40 fruit and nut trees as well as planting vegetable and herb gardens. He intends to share his excess produce at local farmer's markets and at restaurants in the Napa Valley.

Besides the lanai, Craig's favorite features are the 14-ft.-high cathedral ceiling and the clerestory windows in every room, which open up the space, bringing in natural light and positive energy. The rooms are sized perfectly—not too small and not too large, but just right. Even though the new house is barely half the size of his previous house, Craig doesn't feel like he's living in a smaller space—a true testament to the design of this unique home.

A good portion of the wall area in the public spaces is glass, flooding the rooms with ample light. The flooring throughout the main part of the house is light gray, ultra-wide European oak planking.

LEED CERTIFICATION

The U.S. Green Building Council (USGBC) created the LEED for Homes rating system to promote high-performance green design and construction. The goal is to encourage construction of houses that use less energy and fewer resources, produce less waste, and have healthier and more comfortable interior environments.

LEED homes qualify at four levels: Certified, Silver, Gold, and Platinum, based on points earned in a variety of categories. Reaching one of these stringent levels requires commitment on the part of the designer and the builder. Accredited providers work with homeowners, architects, and builders to

assist through the design and construction process and submit the final LEED checklist to the USGBC for certification. Some LEED measures are optional; others are mandatory. In addition, a house must achieve a minimum score on the Home Energy Rating System (HERS) index, a number determined by a blower door test and a test that measures the leakiness of the ductwork. Steve Glenn, the designer of this house, built the first house in the country to achieve LEED Platinum, with 91 points out of a possible 108. To learn more, visit greenhomeguide.org or usgbc.org.

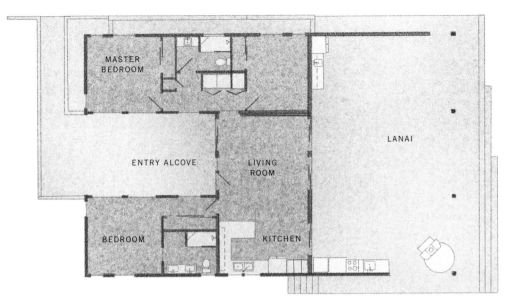

MASTER
BEDROOM

ENTRY ALCOVE

LIVING
ROOM

LANAI

BEDROOM

KITCHEN

The clerestory windows in the master bedroom admit
lots of additional light while also providing privacy.

With a thought for future accessibility, the shower is rimless. Low-flow faucets and a dual-flush toilet save water.

DOWNSIZING FEATURES
• One-floor living
• Barrier-free shower
• Open floor plan
• High ceiling
• Well-placed windows
• Large outdoor space
• Optimal storage space

GREEN FEATURES
• Recycled materials (wood floors,
  bathroom tiles)
• No-VOC paints and stains
• On-demand tankless water heater
• Photovoltaic (PV) system
• ENERGY STAR appliances
• Ductless mini-split heating and
  cooling systems
• Low-flow water fixtures and fittings
• LED lighting
• No turf—all native or culinary plants
• Ceiling fans

The alcove, the main entrance, provides additional protected outdoor space as well as a separation between the two bedrooms. The plan is to finish the area with stabilized decomposed granite in a tan color.

THE RACE RESIDENCE

CONSTRUCTION TYPE:
Site Built

ARCHITECT:
Craig Race Architecture

PHOTOGRAPHER:
Robert Watson
Photography (unless
otherwise noted)

LOCATION:
Toronto, Ontario, Canada

SIZE:
1,200 sq. ft.

FACING PAGE: On this most unusual facade, the cedar shingles arch up toward the peak. In a further twist on the tight infill lot, the front wall angles back to reconcile the different setbacks of the two neighboring houses.

BEFORE THEY BUILT THEIR NEW HOME, ARCHITECT Craig and his wife had been living in a historic 100-year-old house next to their current property for three years (see the top photo on p. 208). They bought the house, which was built on what was originally two lots. At some point in history the two lots were merged, with the unused portion remaining that way because of unstable soil and groundwater issues. In order for Craig to build on this small property he needed to pour footings up to 6 ft. deep in places. Some of the property from the large house was severed to build the new house. After the new house was built, Craig and his wife sold the original house next door to pay for the new one (which also has a separate basement apartment that the couple rents out to help pay the mortgage).

Craig's architectural practice focuses on sustainable, creative, infill development, and he saw in this new construction project the opportunity to showcase his abilities on all those fronts. The old house was drafty and the energy bills were high. When Craig and his wife were preparing to build the new house they wanted to make sure it would be more energy efficient, not only for the lower utility bills but also for the comfort that comes with a well-insulated house. And Craig wanted to demonstrate to his potential clients that he could execute work that is complex and financially advantageous, but also beautiful and environmentally responsible, with a positive impact on the urban environment.

A UNIQUE HOUSE IN A DENSE NEIGHBORHOOD

When Craig and his wife initially purchased the property in 2013, they chose this location because of its proximity to nearby shops, parks, and restaurants. Closeness to those social amenities was more important to them than having a large property. Craig had worked in this area for many years and fell in love with the neighborhood's evolving charm. When they initially looked for a house in this area, it was still affordable and they liked the idea of buying into an up-and coming-community. By the time they moved into the new house at the end of 2017, house prices in the area had risen appreciably and the neighborhood had exploded with new condos, restaurants, and other amenities.

At first glance, the most striking feature of the house is the entry façade. Not only do the cedar shingles arch up dramatically toward the peak of the gable, but one side of the front wall angles back while at the same time tilting forward, almost creating a funhouse effect. But the design is not just to be playful: The houses on either side had different setbacks so the façade is angled to respect the neighbors while also

The living room is filled with natural light from the door and windows that open to the back patio. The marble fireplace, flanked on both sides by built-in red oak shelving, houses a Bio Flame ethanol burner; the marble surround was salvaged from Craig's grandparents' farmhouse.

helping the house to fit in with the aesthetic of the neighborhood.

SMALLER BUT BETTER

To build a house that would generate low utility bills it needed to be superinsulated, exceptionally airtight, and designed for passive heat gain and natural ventilation. After their experience in the drafty, energy-inefficient old house, it was most important that the new house be comfortable and warm in the cold winters. Craig reports that it's possible to stay warm even standing next to a window on the coldest day; the south-facing windows bring in so much passive solar heat gain that it's

ABOVE AND RIGHT: The dropped wood ceiling over the kitchen, clad in warm, red oak paneling, houses the ductwork and plumbing, while the deep windowsill in the dining room is the result of the unique angled façade. The floors are all concrete with an epoxy finish (and embedded radiant heating).

not always necessary to turn on the radiant-floor heating. In the summer, a large deciduous tree shades the windows to prevent overheating.

Craig and his wife took much of their furniture with them from the old house (it wasn't a long journey!). They needed to part with the office furniture when their baby boy arrived during construction; the office in the new house became a nursery. Although the new house is just 100 sq. ft. smaller than the old house, Craig admits that it feels a lot smaller since their first child arrived on the scene.

DOWNSIZING FEATURES
- High ceilings
- Large south-facing windows
- Minimal hallways
- Barrier-free shower

GREEN FEATURES
- Radiant floor heating
- Concrete floors
- Heat recovery ventilator (HRV)
- Low-VOC paint
- ENERGY STAR appliances
- Triple-glazed windows
- Superinsulation
- Infill lot
- Reclaimed materials
- Metal roofing and siding
- Stack effect

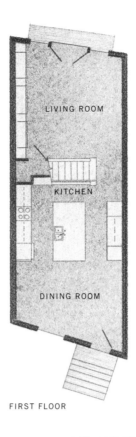

LIVING ROOM

KITCHEN

DINING ROOM

FIRST FLOOR

MASTER BEDROOM

BEDROOM

BEDROOM

SECOND FLOOR

STACK EFFECT

The stack, or chimney, effect is a natural method of ventilation whereby air moves in and out of buildings through a duct or vertical passageway. Hot air is less dense than cold air and rises due to its low pressure. The rising warm air reduces the pressure at the base of the building, sucking cold air into the space from the outside. This is an excellent natural method of cooling a house, particularly for small houses where HVAC equipment space is more limited. In the Race Residence, an operable skylight at the top of the stairs uses the stack effect to naturally ventilate the house.

In the master bedroom, the soaring vaulted ceiling with exposed oak rafter ties makes the room feel much larger than it actually is.

ABOVE AND RIGHT: It's hard to imagine that a house could squeeze into the narrow gap between these houses, but that was the challenge that architect Craig Race overcame. The house above on the right is where Craig and his wife lived before they built the new house (below).

Aside from the cedar shingles on the front, most of the house is clad in standing-seam galvalume, which is durable, low maintenance (it never rusts or fades), and recyclable. The large windows on the south-facing back side allow for passive solar heating.

THERMAL MASS

Thermal mass is generally a solid substance (although it can also be a liquid) that can absorb and store warmth and coolness. Concrete, brick, and stone are examples of high-density materials that have the ability to store and release energy back into a space. In a home, flooring, fireplaces, and walls with a high thermal mass can help to heat and cool the interior space. In the Race Residence, the concrete floors serve as thermal mass.

In winter, solar energy is stored during the day and released at night when the air temperature drops in the house as the material attempts to reach equilibrium with the interior air. This heat released into the house reduces the energy required for heating the interior space. During the summer, heat is absorbed by the solid surfaces, keeping the space more comfortable during the day and reducing the need for air conditioning.

TOTEM HOUSE

CONSTRUCTION TYPE:
Site Built

ARCHITECT:
Reza Aliabadi,
Atelier RZLBD

PHOTOGRAPHER:
Borzu Talaie

LOCATION:
Old East York, Toronto,
Ontario, Canada

SIZE:
1,500 sq. ft.

FACING PAGE: The exterior of the house is a monolithic mass of charcoal brick with two small blocks on the north and south façades clad with wood to create visual contrast. According to architect Reza, "The small wooden corner creates an interesting deception where one imagines the wood to be the core material of the brick mass, like a bitten apple exposing the color of its flesh."

ROBERT AND JOHN WERE LIVING IN A 2,700-SQ.-FT. live/work space in Toronto that was a converted old school warehouse. When the building was slated to become strictly commercial, they had to leave this beloved space and find another place to live in just four months. They temporarily moved into a retrofit loft condo with about 1,000 sq. ft. for less than a year, until they could decide where their next home would be. During that time they visited one of Architect Reza Aliabadi's projects called the Shaft House, and they decided to contact the architect to design and build a new small house to suit their own unique needs and modern, clean aesthetic.

DESIGNING AROUND THE TOTEM

Robert and John are inveterate world travelers, and they wanted their new house to incorporate a space to display the many sculptures and other artifacts they had collected along the way. Architect Reza worked with them to create an unusual vertical gallery that connects the floors like a totem pole and exhibits artwork throughout its height. The house is designed with an open wooden staircase that wraps around this central totem and links the two floors and living roof. Carefully cut niches built within the walls display the many sculptures, which can be seen from several angles while navigating the steps. During the day, the skylight above the staircase illuminates the totem. At night, LED lights installed inside the niches light each art piece. The totem naturally becomes the focal point in the house, visible from every corner on all levels.

URBAN RENEWAL

Robert and John chose this modest emerging neighborhood for its humble identity, easy commute to the city, and proximity to the beach. Although very modest single-story bungalows dominate the area, Reza saw this house as an opportunity to revive the "tired landscape and set a standard for the new contemporary homes that are surfacing."

Robert and John wanted the house to be as sustainable and maintenance-free as possible. On the front of the house permeable paving lines the driveway, allowing storm water to permeate through the ground. Permeable paving continues in the rear, and there is also a wood deck that is sealed so it rarely needs to be treated.

PASSIVE ENERGY STRATEGIES

The house is designed to rely largely on passive energy sources with the goal of minimizing fossil fuel usage. Extensive glazing on the south

ABOVE: The totem in the center of the house, which serves as a vertical gallery, separates the living and dining room areas from the kitchen. The flooring is scored concrete.

RIGHT: An open wood staircase connects the three stories circulating around the totem. This configuration allows the viewer to observe the many pieces of artwork inside the tower from different angles. The art pieces are carefully placed in designated niches, illuminated with a skylight by day and LED lights at night.

ABOVE: The owners wanted an uncluttered look throughout the house. The gas burner with downdraft ventilation, concealed cabinetry, and minimal appliances maintain the clean geometric look of the kitchen.

LEFT: The en suite bathroom and master bedroom are open to each other, defined only by the marble tile floor that separates the bath and shower from the hardwood floor in the rest of the bedroom area. The shower stall is walled with clear glass on three sides, while the freestanding bathtub sits in the corner of the room with a view to the treetops in the courtyard.

side of the house optimizes solar energy, while limited glazing on the north minimizes energy loss. Excellent daylighting is created by the placement of windows and the skylight above the floating staircase. The brick exterior creates thermal mass, which helps to keep the house warm on cold winter days and cool in the hot summer. High-efficiency appliances and furnace along with LED lighting also minimize electrical use. Natural ventilation of the house is made possible through the stack effect (see p. 206) created by the skylight above the top of the totem. The windows are all operable, also allowing for the natural transfer of air.

FIRST FLOOR

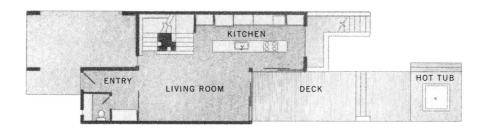

ENTRY

KITCHEN

LIVING ROOM

DECK

HOT TUB

SECOND FLOOR

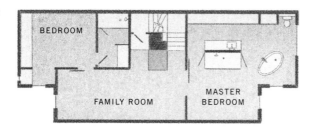

BEDROOM

FAMILY ROOM

MASTER BEDROOM

ROOF

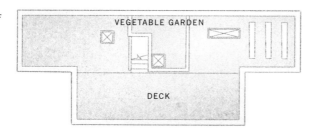

VEGETABLE GARDEN

DECK

DOWNSIZING FEATURES
- Multipurpose spaces
- No hallways
- High ceilings
- Limited partition walls
- Multiple outdoor spaces

GREEN FEATURES
- Extensive glazing on south façade
- Stack effect
- Permeable paving
- Infill lot
- LED lights
- Natural daylighting
- Brick walls for thermal mass
- Living roof
- Passive cooling

PERMEABLE PAVING

Permeable paving provides a solid surface for vehicles while allowing surface water, such as rainwater and snowmelt, to permeate through it, naturally filtering out pollutants and recharging the water table. There are a variety of permeable paving materials available, including porous grass pavers, gravel, crushed stone, pervious concrete, porous asphalt, and shells in beach locations. Though these materials can cost as much as 40% more than traditional asphalt surfaces, they are generally maintenance-free and better for the environment. For additional information visitepa.gov/soakuptherain/soak-rain-permeable-pavement.

ABOVE: Flanked on both sides by houses that show the aesthetic of the past; the Totem House is a striking example of the rejuvenation of the future for this area.

LEFT: Maintenance-free, permeable paving continues at the back of the house, where it combines with wood decking and a hot tub.

GRANNY PAD

CONSTRUCTION TYPE:
On-Site ADU

ARCHITECT:
Best Practice
Architecture

BUILDER:
Kable Design Build

PHOTOGRAPHER:
Sozinho Imagery

LOCATION:
Seattle, Wash.

SIZE:
571 sq. ft.

ILGA AND KYLE'S GRANNY, A VERY HEALTHY AND spry 93-year-old, was living in her own 3,500-sq.-ft. home, but after her husband's long-term illness and eventual passing, she no longer had the need for a larger home. So Granny moved in with her daughter and son-in-law. Because most dwellings are not designed and built to accommodate multifamily living situations, the living arrangement was not ideal. She desperately wanted her own space with kitchen and laundry so she could live independently nearby but not interfere with the family's routine. She eventually moved between her three kids' households, living within each child's home over the years until the opportunity to build a backyard ADU surfaced: Ilga and Kyle leveraged their large backyard and the existing one-car garage to build exactly what they wanted. This proved to be a lower-cost option than buying a new house along with the headaches that go along with a major move. An additional benefit was that Granny could help with their baby, born in November 2018.

DOWNSIZING BUT EYE-OPENING

Downsizing from her larger home proved to be a difficult experience for Granny, but it was also revelatory. Living in a world where stuff is so easy to obtain, store, and collect over and over again, she didn't realize she had accrued, for example, three unused couches, multiple sets of flatware, and banker's boxes full of papers and documents. She was delighted when it was gone and happy that she'd never have to haul these things from house to house again. Most of the items that were not tossed went to Goodwill.

Life with fewer possessions is much simpler for Granny, and she reports feeling a general sense of lightness. Now that she has culled through a lifetime of accumulated possessions, she has the right balance of nostalgia and necessity, with everything important easily accessible, not hidden away in some mystery box in the basement.

WORKING WITH BEST PRACTICE

The couple found the architectural firm Best Practice on the recommendation of Kyle's previous employer. Their aesthetic and simple, smart designs appealed to the couple, and Best Practice was extremely collaborative and helpful in anticipating potential design issues: how to retain privacy for the main house while offering a comfortable, light, and airy space for Granny's use; how to think forward to Granny's possible mobility issues by keeping the space ADA-compliant; and how to maximize daylight on the eastern downhill slope that tends to be prone to shade most of the day.

FACING PAGE: There are two entrances to the house. The lower level (shown here) provides easy entry for Granny, while the loft leads out to a private deck (visible in the photo on p. 221).

ABOVE: All of Granny's needs are accommodated on one level with a bedroom, bathroom, kitchen, and sitting area. The white walls give this house a spacious feel, and the concrete floors are low-maintenance.

RIGHT: The loft area beyond and above the bed area (behind the red cabinet) could be converted to a sleeping loft in the future.

One of the main challenges in building in this location was the existing hill in the rear of the house. Ilga and Kyle wanted to make the most of the usable yard space while creating a shareable area on their upper lot and also a private outdoor space for the Granny Pad—including a private garden where Granny could continue her favorite pastime of gardening. They accomplished this by building into the backyard slope and creating a loft space that has its own door exiting to the top of the hill.

The ADU took just six months to build. It is hardly noticeable from the street even though it provides a second household on the property. Ilga and Kyle say that somehow their backyard looks bigger and more accessible with the addition of

the Granny Pad. Once inside, the space feels roomy and grand for such a small structure. The high ceilings make it appear twice the size it is, and the unique design elements, such as stained plywood panels, add visual interest to the home.

LIVING BETWEEN TWO HOUSEHOLDS

The family has a perfect, symbiotic and balanced routine between the two households. Everyone comes together in the courtyard between the two houses for morning coffee, or they find their private quiet space at each other's home at a moment's notice. The dog even has an increased quality of life, with breakfast at two households every morning!

RIGHT: The high ceiling with exposed rafters and the well-placed skylights and windows make the small house seem larger than it is. Open shelving creates easy access to kitchen items, and small appliances provide a compact but well-functioning kitchen area.

BELOW: The exterior door in the sleeping area was initially a large window, but the owners wanted a quick exit for safety and also easy access to the upper lot. The Dutch door was added as visual interest, with the bottom half of the door lining up with the gray-painted wall. The door's upper window offers a good view of the fern garden beyond the side walkway.

MINI APPLIANCES

Many appliance manufacturers have begun to offer smaller sizes of popular models that are appropriate for use in compact spaces, such as small-footprint houses, apartments, and tiny houses. All of the appliances in the Granny Pad are 24 in. wide (stove, refrigerator, washer and dryer). They were chosen both to save space and because Granny didn't need anything larger. In general, using smaller appliances promotes accessibility, leaves room for more storage, and can increase counter space. The mini appliances used in the Granny Pad are from Blomberg Appliances (blombergappliances.com).

ABOVE AND LEFT: The garage of this house in the Maple Leaf neighborhood just north of Seattle's University district was converted to a backyard ADU, so Granny could comfortably age in place and also help with childcare for this growing family. The garage was previously used for storage.

The garage door was removed and the old structure was converted to an entry, kitchen, and sitting area (the building at right). An addition was added with a bedroom, bathroom, and loft area above (the building at left).

DOWNSIZING FEATURES
- One-floor living
- Barrier-free shower
- Open floor plan
- High ceiling
- Well-placed windows and skylights
- Mini appliances

GREEN FEATURES
- Small footprint
- Energy-efficient windows and appliances
- Low-VOC finishes
- Parking strip replaced with a garden
- Daylighting

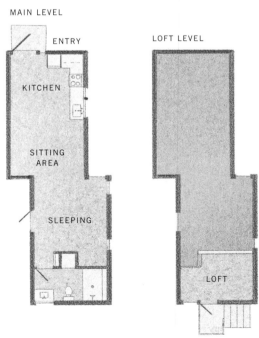

MAIN LEVEL

ENTRY

KITCHEN

SITTING AREA

SLEEPING

LOFT LEVEL

LOFT

ERICKSON HOUSE

CONSTRUCTION TYPE:
Panelized

ARCHITECT/ MANUFACTURER:
Stillwater Dwellings

PHOTOGRAPHER:
Jeff Amram Photography

LOCATION:
Whidbey Island, Wash.

SIZE:
1,200 sq. ft.

THERE'S A QUOTE WRITTEN ON THE CHALKBOARD IN Molly and Joe Erickson's kitchen that says "You can't get any closer to heaven than Bells Beach." This pretty much sums up how the couple feels about living in their new oceanside cabin near Langley, Wash.

Bells Beach was developed by Joe's grandfather (Grandpa Bell of the legendary quote above) in the 1930s, and Joe's parents built a summer cabin there in 1953; Joe himself practically grew up on Bells Beach. He bought his own cabin just down the road from his parents' place in 1997 and always described it as "the weekend project" because it looked a little like a do-it-yourself job, put together over many years. It was admittedly cute, but somewhat drafty and dark with some awkward spaces (just one small closet in the whole house, room only for two kitchen cabinets, a very narrow bathroom with barely room to turn around in, and a doorless bedroom because there was no way to hang one).

After Joe married Molly in 2010 they began talking about replacing the old cabin with a modern, warm cabin with lots of light: small but with plenty of space for friends and family to gather to enjoy the fresh crab and clams caught just feet from the front door. While researching designs and builders they discovered Stillwater Dwellings and chose one of their panelized house designs, where the main components are shipped from a factory and assembled on site, saving time and money. The house was built in just six months.

Energy efficiency was a priority for the owners, and Stillwater delivered. The hydronic radiant heating system, high-efficiency windows, and a hybrid insulation system consisting of closed-cell spray insulation along with fiberglass insulation provide a high R-value at a reasonable cost.

CHALLENGES TO BUILDING BY THE WATER

The project presented some design and engineering changes due to its proximity to the water. Shoreline regulations as well as federal flood plain guidelines were among the factors that dictated the plan. The house also had to be designed to satisfy Molly and Joe's wish for a one-story age-in-place residence that required minimal maintenance. Transitional spaces between indoors and out were designed to eliminate any unwanted steps, and the floor plan was kept open, especially in the public areas of the house.

MAKING THEIR BEACH HOME THEIR PRIMARY HOME

This isn't the only house in the book that evolved from a weekend/ vacation getaway to a full-time residence; this is a pattern we see recur-

With minimal maintenance in mind, this house on Puget Sound was designed with fiber cement siding and an EPDM roof (a highly durable synthetic rubber roofing membrane).

In the kitchen, a floor-to-ceiling painted chalkboard is used for decoration and to-do lists. It is also signed by visitors to the house. The kitchen countertops are quartz and all appliances are ENERGY STAR rated. The reclaimed barn door is visible in the hallway, which leads to the mudroom. The door was made from one of the exterior doors of their old cabin.

ring time and again as the downsizing bug grabs hold. After the new cabin was built in 2016, Joe and Molly were spending more time there than at their much larger 3,300-sq.-ft. home in Seattle. They realized that the money and effort to maintain both houses could be better spent elsewhere—in traveling, for example. So in May 2018 they sold their Seattle house where Joe had lived for 30-plus years and moved to Bells Beach to live full time in their new beloved beach cabin.

BARN DOORS

Barn doors are increasingly popular in homes today. They are typically one or two large panels hung from a heavy bar mounted above a door opening. The door moves along the bar using a set of rollers attached to the top of the frame. Often, antique or reclaimed doors are repurposed as barn doors though sometimes they are new. Barn doors can be entrance doors, closet doors, and room dividers; they can also be used for less traditional purposes, such as concealing a television or storage space. Barn doors are available in a variety of styles from rustic to modern and in a wide range of materials and colors. One of the advantages of barn doors, particularly in small houses, is the space they save: Barn doors take up less room than doors that swing in or out on hinges.

TOP AND ABOVE: Sliding glass doors open up the house to natural ventilation, daylighting, and beautiful ocean views. These large glass doors and clerestory windows give the house a much more expansive feeling, an important feature in a small house.

PATIO

KITCHEN

LIVING
ROOM

DINING
ROOM

ENTRY

MUDROOM

BEDROOM

MASTER BEDROOM

DOWNSIZING FEATURES
- One-floor living
- Low-maintenance materials
- Minimal hallways
- High ceilings
- Barrier-free shower
- Expansive outdoor space

GREEN FEATURES
- Fiber cement siding
- Deep overhangs
- EPDM roof
- Hydronic radiant heating system
- Whole-house ventilation system
- Superinsulation
- Recycled materials

RADIANT HEAT

Radiant heat, both hydronic and electric, provides clean, even heat, warming objects in the room rather than the air, as forced-air heating systems do. Radiant systems are noise-free, provide greater comfort with heat spread evenly throughout the area, and can be zoned so only the areas being used are heated. Unlike forced-air systems, no particulates and pollutants are introduced into the environment from the blown air, making it a healthier form of heating. Radiant heating systems are embedded in flooring, ceiling, or wall panels and can also be used to melt snow on driveways and sidewalks. Hydronic or hot-water radiant systems can also heat a pool, spa, or domestic hot water.

Large roof overhangs at the entrance and around the periphery of the house protect those entering and leaving while also providing a place for wet shoes and umbrellas.

ABOVE: One of the great features of this house is the proximity to the ocean and the magnificent views. The concrete patio on the northeast-facing side expands the living space, providing additional dining and sitting areas overlooking the water.

RIGHT: The side of the house that faces the Saratoga Passage, which is part of the Salish Sea, has multiple sliding glass doors to take advantage of the water views. Operable clerestory windows add additional light and natural ventilation. The sloped roof creates a higher ceiling on the ocean-facing side of the house, expanding the amount of light and fresh air coming into the house.

RESOURCES

EDMONDS HOUSE
pp. 14–19

ARCHITECT/MANUFACTURER
Stillwater Dwellings
http://stillwaterdwellings.com

CONTRACTOR
Jim Anderson, Adobe
Construction, Inc.

PHOTOGRAPHER
Jeff Amram Photography
www.jeffamram.com

SUPPLIERS
JamesHardie (concrete panel
siding)
www.jameshardie.com

Milgard Windows & Doors
(vinyl windows)
www.milgard.com

Sierra Pacific Windows
(sliding glass doors)
www.sierrapacificwindows.com

Rogue Valley Door (entry door)
www.roguevalleydoor.com

JELD-WEN (interior doors)
www.jeld-wen.com

Baldwin (door hardware)
www.baldwinhardware.com

Therma-Tru Doors (garage
door)
www.therma-tru.com

Velux (skylights)
www.veluxusa.com

Caesarstone (countertops)
www.caesarstoneus.com

IKEA (kitchen cabinets)
www.ikea.com

NEW STREET HOUSE
pp. 20–25

ARCHITECT
Cooter Ramsey, Allison
Ramsey Architects
www.allisonramseyarchitect
.com

BUILDER
Allen Patterson, Patterson
Residential
http://allenpatterson
residential.com

PHOTOGRAPHER
Sandy Dimke
www.dimkephoto.com

SUPPLIERS
Marvin (windows)
www.marvin.com

Sherwin-Williams (paint)
www.sherwin-williams.com

Trane (mini-split)
www.trane.com

JamesHardie (siding)
www.jameshardie.com

CertainTeed (roofing)
www.certainteed.com

Mirabelle (sink)
www.mirabelleproducts.com

TOTO (sink)
www.totousa.com

American Standard (toilet)
www.americanstandard-us
.com

Thermador (appliances)
www.thermador.com

Danby (wine cooler)
www.danby.com

Adorne (undercounter lighting
system by Legrand)
www.legrand.us/adorne

MADISON PASSIVE
pp. 26–31

ARCHITECT
Tessa Smith, Artisans Group
https://artisansgroup.com

BUILDERS
Randy Foster, Brian Colbert,
Owen Martin, Artisans Group

PHOTOGRAPHER
Poppi Photography
www.poppiphoto.com

INTERIOR DESIGNER
Brenda Fritsch, Artisans
Group

SUPPLIERS
Zola Windows (triple-glazed
windows)
www.zolawindows.com

Beech Tree Woodworks
(cabinetry)
http://beechtreecustom
cabinets.com

Intellihot (Combi tankless
radiant heat and on-demand
hot water heater)
www.intellihot.com

Zehnder (HRV)
https://zehnderamerica.com

Bosch (washer, condensing
dryer)
www.bosch-home.com

Fisher & Paykel (French door
refrigerator)
www.fisherpaykel.com

Miele (dishwasher)
www.mieleusa.com

DCS (stovetop, oven)
www.dcsappliances.com

Louis Poulsen (PH50 dining
nook lights)
www.louispoulsen.com

GROUNDSWELL HOUSE
pp. 32–39

ARCHITECT
Solterre Design
www.solterre.com

BUILDER
Jim Morash Construction
www.morashconstruction.com

PHOTOGRAPHER
Adam Cornick, Acorn Art &
Photography
www.acornart.net

SUPPLIERS
Rheem (heat pump hot-water
heater)
www.rheem.com

Fujitsu (air-source heat pump)
www.fujitsugeneral.com

Zehnder (HRV)
https://zehnderamerica.com

Stûv (high-efficiency
woodstove [Stûv 30])
https://stuvamerica.com/en

Jøtul (high-efficiency
woodstove [Jotul F602])
https://jotul.com/us

DUXTON Windows & Doors
(triple-glazed windows)
www.duxtonwindows.com

Sunspace (sunroom windows)
https://sunspacesunrooms
.com

KitchenAid (appliances)
www.kitchenaid.com

Big Ass Fans (ceiling fans)
www.bigassfans.com

HOUSE ON WALDEN POND
pp. 40–45

DESIGNER/MANUFACTURER/
BUILDER
Yankee Barn Homes
www.yankeebarnhomes.com

PHOTOGRAPHER
Bob Gothard
www.marthasvineyard
architecturalphotographer.com

SUPPLIERS
Peak Co Roofing (asphalt
shingle roofing, cedar shingle
siding)
https://peakcompanyroofing
.com

Marvin (windows)
www.marvin.com

Arsenault Flooring (white oak
rift- and quartersawn flooring)
Maynard, Mass.

Thermador (appliances)
www.thermador.com

Bosch (oven)
www.bosch-home.com

MORTON HOUSE
pp. 46–51

ARCHITECT
Hicks Stone, Stone
Architecture LLC
www.stone-architecture.com

CARPENTER/CONTRACTOR
Bernie Plonski
Canaan, Conn.

PHOTOGRAPHER
Randy O'Rourke
www.rorphotos.com

SUPPLIERS
Mitsubishi (mini-splits)
www.mitsubishicomfort.com

RenewAire (ERV)
www.renewaire.com

Benjamin Moore (low-VOC
paint)
www.benjaminmoore.com

Wolf (induction stovetop)
www.subzero-wolf.com

Rockwool (mineral wool
insulation)
www.rockwool.com

INTUS (windows)
www.intuswindows.com

Everlast Roofing, Inc. (metal
roofing)
https://everlastroofing.com

Ian Ingersoll (kitchen stools)
www.ianingersoll.com

Sonia (showerhead)
www.sonia-sa.com/en/

Duravit (vanity, sink, toilet)
www.duravit.us

Keuco (wall mirror)
www.keuco.co.gb

Sigma (faucet, showerhead)
www.sigmafaucet.com

Design Within Reach (sofa)
www.dwr.com

SKIDMORE PASSIVHAUS
pp. 52–59

ARCHITECT/GENERAL
CONTRACTOR
Jeff Stern, In Situ Architecture
www.insituarchitecture.net

PHOTOGRAPHER
Jeremy Bittermann
www.bittermannphotography.com

SUPPLIERS
Zola Windows (windows,
doors)
www.zolawindows.com

HELLA (exterior Venetian
blinds)
www.hella.info/en

Zehnder (HRV)
www.zehnderamerica.com

Abet Laminati (laminate
countertops)
http://abetlaminati.com/en/

Frigidaire (induction cooktop)
www.frigidaire.com

Fisher & Paykel (refrigerator)
www.fisherpaykel.com/us

Blomberg (dishwasher)
www.blombergappliances.com

Asko (washer, condensing
dryer)
www.askona.com

LONGLEAF HOUSE
pp. 60–65

DESIGNER
Esposito Design
www.espositodesign.net

BUILDER
Brandon Construction
www.brandonbuilding.com

PHOTOGRAPHER
Joel Esposito

SUPPLIERS
Marvin (windows)
www.marvin.com

Rogue Valley (solid-wood
exterior doors)
www.roguevalleydoor.com

Sherwin-Williams (paint)
www.sherwin-williams.com

Trane (high-efficiency HVAC)
www.trane.com

Gulf Coast Supply &
Manufacturing (GulfLok
metal roofing)
www.gulfcoastsupply.com

JamesHardie (fiber cement lap
siding)
www.jameshardie.com

Huber ZIPsystem (sheathing,
tape, liquid flashing)
www.huberwood.com/
zipsystem

Huber Advantech (sheathing
for subfloor and roof deck)
www.huberwood.com/
advantech

True Residential (refrigerators)
https://true-residential.com

Silestone (quartz countertops)
www.silestoneusa.com

Isokern (modular fireplace)
http://earthcore.co/isokern

GE Appliances (induction
range)
www.geappliances.com

Kohler (farmhouse sink)
www.us.kohler.com

PINWHEEL ADU
pp. 66–71

ARCHITECT
Scott Mooney, SRG
Partnership, Inc.
www.srgpartnership.com

CONTRACTOR
TaylorSmith Sustainable
Construction
www.taylorsmithsc.com

PHOTOGRAPHER
Olivia Ashton
http://oliviaashtonphotography
.com

SUPPLIERS
Sustainable Northwest Wood
(FSC-certified western red
cedar siding)
www.snwwood.com

Milgard Windows & Doors
(Essence Series windows)
www.milgard.com

Kohler (bathroom fixtures)
www.us.kohler.com

Perch (couch)
www.perchfurniture.com

APPLIANCES
www.compactappliance.com

Avanti (refrigerator)
www.avantiproducts.com

Amana (stove, oven)
www.amana.com

Frigidaire (dishwasher)
www.frigidaire.com

LG (ventless washer/dryer
combo)
www.lg.com/us

MAINE CAMP REBOOT
pp. 72–79

ARCHITECT/BUILDER
Gunther Kragler, GO Logic
www.gologic.us

PHOTOGRAPHER
Josh Gerritsen Media
http://joshgerritsen.com

SUPPLIERS
Rockwool (mineral wool
insulation)
www.rockwool.com

GO Logic (patented high-
performance slab on grade)
www.gologic.us

Kneer-Südfenster (windows,
doors)
www.kneer-suedfenster.de/en

Lunos (HRV)
www.lunos.de/en/

NuImage Awnings
www.nuimageawnings.com

Whirlpool (washer, dryer)
www.whirlpool.com

Rakks (kitchen and living
room open-shelving system)
http://rakks.com/shelf-
support-brackets

Sundog Solar (solar system)
http://sundog.solar

Rinnai heater (propane space
heater)
www.rinnai.us

IKEA (cabinets)
www.ikea.com

Connecticut Screen Works
(screen system for porch)
http://connscreen.com

THE BEACH COTTAGE
pp. 80–85

DESIGNER/DEVELOPER
Steve Hoiles
www.surfsideprojects.com

PHOTOGRAPHER
Darren Bradley/OTTO
www.darrenbradley
photography.com

SUPPLIERS
ANDlight (pendant fixture)
https://andlight.ca/
pipeline-125

Fisher & Paykel (appliances)
www.fisherpaykel.com

Metropolitan (engineered hardwood flooring)
www.metrofloors.com

Thermory (rear wood decking)
www.thermoryusa.com

Pental Quartz (countertops)
www.pentalquartz.com

Western Window Systems (sliding glass doors)
www.westernwindowsystems.com

Grohe (kitchen faucet)
www.grohe.us

Kohler (kitchen sink)
www.us.kohler.com

Duravit (master bath washbasin, wall-hung dual-flush toilet)
www.duravit.us

Hans Grohe (outdoor and indoor shower)
www.hansgrohe-usa.com

HERON ROCK COTTAGE
pp. 86–93

ARCHITECT/MANUFACTURER
Lindal Cedar Homes
www.lindal.com

DESIGN AND PLANNING
Michael Harris, Warmmodern Living
https://warmmodernliving.com

ON-SITE CONSTRUCTION
Northwest Stout Construction, Freeland, Wash.

LANDSCAPE ARCHITECT
Masa Mizuno

PHOTOGRAPHER
Patrick Barta
www.bartaphoto.com

SUPPLIERS
Milgard Windows & Doors (Montecito vinyl-framed windows)
www.milgard.com

Simpson Door Company (exterior and interior doors)
www.simpsondoor.com

Baldwin (door hardware)
www.baldwinhardware.com

AEP Span (corrugated steel siding)
www.aepspan.com

Fisher & Paykel (refrigerator/freezer)
www.fisherpaykel.com/us

CARRIAGE HOUSE
pp. 94–99

ARCHITECT
Shawn Buehler, Bennett Frank McCarthy Architects, Inc.
https://bfmarch.com

GENERAL CONTRACTOR
Owner

PHOTOGRAPHER
Bennett Frank McCarthy Architects, Inc.

SUPPLIERS
Weather Shield Windows & Doors (windows)
www.weathershield.com

Mitsubishi Electric (ductless mini-splits)
www.mitsubishicomfort.com

Farrow & Ball (paint and wallpaper)
www.farrow-ball.com

HERON HAUS
pp. 100–105

ARCHITECT
Tessa Smith, Artisans Group
https://artisansgroup.com

INTERIOR DESIGNER
Brenda Fritsch, Artisans Group

CONSTRUCTION MANAGERS
Randy Foster, Dave Canfield, Owen Martin, Artisans Group

PHOTOGRAPHER
Poppi Photography
www.poppiphoto.com

SUPPLIERS
Zola Windows (windows, doors)
www.zolawindows.com

Zehnder (HRV)
https://zehnderamerica.com

Fujitsu (heat pump)
www.fujitsu-general.com

Columbia (kitchen cabinets)
www.columbiacabinets.com

Bosch (appliances)
www.bosch-home.com

Liebherr (refrigerator)
https://home.liebherr.com

Lumens (lights)
www.lumens.com

YLighting (lights)
www.ylighting.com

Rodda (paint)
www.roddapaint.com

The Shade Store (roller shades)
www.theshadestore.com

LAKE SUPERIOR HOUSE
pp. 106–113

ARCHITECT
Rosemary McMonigal, FAIA, LEED AP, CID
Nick Dellwo, Phil Hofstad, and James Arentson, AIA
McMonigal Architects
www.mcmonigal.com

BUILDER
Cedar Brook Construction
www.cedarbrookwi.com
Ann and Pete Brownlee

PHOTOGRAPHER
Greg Page Photography
https://gregpagephotography.com

SUPPLIERS
Thermomass (concrete walls)
http://thermomass.com

Feeney (railing)
www.feeneyinc.com

Interior Rail System (railing)
Custom designed by McMonigal Architects
www.mcmonigal.com

Energy Panel Structures (SIPs)
www.epsbuildings.com

Firestone Building Products (steel roof)
www.firestonebpco.com

Therma-Tru Doors (exterior doors)
www.thermatru.com

H Window (windows)
www.hwindow.com

Eco by Cosentino (kitchen and bath counters)
http://ecobycosentino.com/usa

Samsung (refrigerator)
www.samsung.com/us

Whirlpool (stove, microwave/hood)
www.whirlpool.com

Lopi Stoves (woodstove)
www.lopistoves.com

FinnSisu (sauna)
https://finnsisu.com

Juno Lighting Group (lights)
https://juno.acuitybrands.com

Hi-Lite Mfg. Co. (decorative lights)
www.hilitemfg.com

WEE BARN
pp. 114–119

ARCHITECT
Geoffrey C. Warner, Alchemy
www.weehouse.com

GENERAL CONTRACTOR
Matt Haney, Carina Construction
https://carinaconstruction.com

MANUFACTURER
Apex Homes
www.apexhomesofpa.com

PHOTOGRAPHER
Geoffrey C. Warner

SUPPLIERS
IKEA (cabinets)
www.ikea.com

Daltile (flooring)
www.daltile.com

Andersen Windows & Doors (windows)
www.andersenwindows.com

Richlite (paper countertops)
https://richlite.com

Vigo (pull-out kitchen faucet)
www.vigoindustries.com

Leviton (light switches)
www.leviton.com

The Modern Fan Co (ceiling fan)
https://modernfan.com

Duravit (bathtub)
www.duravit.us

Nest (thermostat, smoke detector)
https://nest.com

Pratt & Lambert Paints (paint)
www.prattandlambert.com

Superior Walls (foundation)
www.superiorwalls.com

Kohler (dual-flush toilet)
www.us.kohler.com

Bosch (dual-fuel slide-in range)
www.bosch-home.com

ASKO (dishwasher)
www.askona.com/dishwashers

Frigidaire (refrigerator)
www.frigidaire.com

Electrolux (washer, dryer)
www.electroluxappliances.com

Drolet (Deco woodstove)
www.drolet.ca

Gatco (stainless bath and towel bars)
www.gatco-inc.com

Uponor (in-floor hydronic heat)
www.uponor-usa.com

RIVERVIEW HOUSE
pp. 120–125

ARCHITECT
Alterstudio Architecture
http://alterstudio.net

CONTRACTOR
R Builders LLC
https://rbuildersllc.com

LANDSCAPE DESIGNER
Alisa West, Westshop
http://westshopdesign.com

STRUCTURAL ENGINEER
Scott Williamson

PHOTOGRAPHER
Casey Dunn
https://caseydunn.net

SUPPLIERS
WAC Lighting
www.waclighting.com

MinkaAire (ceiling fans, dehumidifier)
www.minkagroup.net

Palladio Wide Plank (white oak flooring)
www.palladioplank.com

Benjamin Moore (paint)
www.benjaminmoore.com

Caeserstone (kitchen and bath countertops)
www.caesarstoneus.com

McIntyre Tile (glazed Delta Blue tile for master bath floor)
www.mcintyre-tile.com

Hakatai Tile (master bath shower wall)
www.hakatai.com

Trikeenan (tile)
https://trikeenan.com

Brewster Home Fashions (wallpaper in laundry room)
www.brewsterwallcovering.com

Liebherr (refrigerator and freezer)
www.liebherr.com

Bosch (cooktop, wall oven, dishwasher)
www.bosch-home.com

Kohler (sinks)
www.us.kohler.com

Newport Brass (faucet)
www.newport-brass-store.com

Grohe (faucets, shower fixtures)
www.grohe.us/en_us

TOTO (toilet)
www.totousa.com

Rinnai (tankless hot water heater)
www.rinnai.us

Ram Windows
www.ramwindows.com

Western Window Systems (triple sliding door)
www.westernwindowsystems.com

Mitsubishi Electric (HVAC)
www.mitsubishicomfort.com

Positive Energy (VRF HVAC equipment)
https://positiveenergy.pro

A HOME IN FLETCHER PLACE
pp. 126–131

ARCHITECT/BUILDER
Patrick Kestner, AIA,
Clete Kunce, AIA
ONE 10 STUDIO
http://one10studio.com

PHOTOGRAPHER
Lesle Lane
Studio 13 Photography
www.studio13online.com

SUPPLIERS
Pella (Impervia windows)
www.pella.com

Hanex (solid-surface counters)
www.hanexsolidsurfaces.com

Juno (lighting)
https://juno.acuitybrands.com

Artemide (lighting)
www.artemide.com

THE COTTAGE AT EXTOWN FARM
pp. 132–137

ARCHITECT
David D. Harlan Architects
www.ddharlanarchitects.com

INTERIOR DESIGN
A. Defne Veral Interiors, LLC
www.adveralinteriors.com

LANDSCAPE ARCHITECT
Devore Associates
https://devoreassoc.com

CIVIL ENGINEER
Landtech
www.landtechconsult.com

STRUCTURAL ENGINEER
GNCB Consulting Engineers, P.C.
www.gncbengineers.com

BUILDER
EM Rose Builders
https://emrose.net

SUPPLIERS
Benjamin Moore (paint)
www.benjaminmoore.com

JennAir (refrigerator)
https://v1.jennair.com

Lepage (windows)
www.lepagemillwork.com/en-ca

Viking (range)
www.vikingrange.com

Bosch (dishwasher)
www.bosch-home.com

Lutron (lighting fixtures)
www.lutron.com

Waterworks (fittings, fixtures)
www.waterworks.com

SOLTERRE CONCEPT HOUSE
pp. 138–145

ARCHITECT
Solterre Design
www.solterre.com

PASSIVE HOUSE CONSULTING
Passive Design Solutions
www.passivedesign.ca

LEED PROVIDE/RATER
ThermalWise
www.thermalwise.ca

MECHANICAL/ENERGY CONSULTANT
Equilibrium Engineering
www.equilibrium-engineering.ca

LANDSCAPE AND GREEN ROOF CONSULTANT
Outside! Planning & Design Studio
www.outsideplanning.com

STRUCTURAL ENGINEER
Sherwood Enterprises
sherwoodinc@eastlink.ca

ENERGUIDE ENERGY CONSULTANT
Sustainable Housing
www.sustainablehousing.ca

LAND SURVEYOR
Berrigan Surveys Ltd.
http://berrigansurveys.ca

PHOTOGRAPHER
Adam Cornick, Acorn Art & Photography
www.acornart.net

SUPPLIERS
TrueFoam Ltd. (EPS foundation insulation)
www.truefoam.com
Thermo-Cell Industries (cellulose insulation)
www.thermocell.com

CertainTeed (cement board siding)
www.certainteed.com

Miller Group (recycled glass for slab and septic field)
www.millergroup.ca

South Shore Ready Mix (concrete mix with recycled glass)
www.ssreadymix.ns.ca

Eco-House (exterior silicate paint)
www.eco-house.com

Accurate Dorwin (fiberglass windows)
www.accuratedorwin.com

UtimateAir (ERV)
www.ultimateair.com

WELServer (monitoring equipment)
www.welserver.com

ThermalWood Canada (torrefied wood siding)
www.thermalwoodcanada.com

J & S Paints Ltd. (Glidden ICI paint)
www.jspaints.com

Thermo Homes Inc. (Noritz Eco propane boiler)
www.thermohomes.ca

Thermo Dynamics (solar thermal system)
www.thermo-dynamics.com

Wittus (woodstove)
www.wittus.com

Musquodoboit Valley Quality Sod (living roof RTF sod supplier)
www.mvqs.ca

VicWest Steel (galvalume roofing with 30% recycled content)
https://vicwest.com

OutBack Power (solar PV controls)
www.outbackpower.com

Sun Frost (high-efficiency refrigerator/freezer)
www.sunfrost.com

LIVE OAK HOUSE
pp. 146–151

ARCHITECT/GENERAL CONTRACTOR

James Rory Reynolds
Rory Reynolds + Associates
www.roryraa.com

INTERIOR DESIGNER/ PHOTOGRAPHER

Mandy Cheng Design
www.mandychengdesign.com

SUPPLIERS

Therma-Tru Door (swinging doors)
www.thermatru.com

Andersen Windows & Doors (windows)
www.andersenwindows.com

GAF (EverGuard TPO roof)
www.gaf.com/en-us

Clopay (garage doors)
www.clopaydoor.com

Sherwin-Williams (paint)
www.sherwin-williams.com

Bocci (stairwell chandelier)
www.bocci.ca

Honeywell (programmable thermostat)
www.honeywellstore.com

Sonos (whole house audio)
www.sonos.com

PGT Custom Windows & Doors (sliding doors)
www.pgtwindows.com/doors

Bear Metal Welding & Fabrication, Inc. (custom steel railing)
www.bearmetalwelding.com

Fisher & Paykel (appliances)
www.fisherpaykel.com

Kohler (faucet fixtures)
www.us.kohler.com

Schlage (interior door knobs)
www.schlage.com

Emtek (entry door hardware)
https://emtek.com

CASCADE MOUNTAIN HOUSE
pp. 152–159

ARCHITECT

FabCab
http://fabcab.com

BUILDER

James Hall and Associates
www.jameshallandassociates .com

PHOTOGRAPHER

Dale Lang, NW Architectural Photography
www.nwphoto.net

INTERIOR DESIGN

Tracy Ronaldson, Liz Davis ecd Design LLC, Edmonds, Wash.

SUPPLIERS

Frank Lumber (entry door)
www.franklumber.com/ kylemont

Andersen Windows & Doors
www.andersenwindows.com

Northwest Door (garage door)
www.nwdusa.com

Bosch (refrigerator, wall oven, microwave drawer, induction stovetop)
www.bosch-home.com

Zephyr (range hood)
https://zephyronline.com

Fisher & Paykel (double-drawer dishwasher)
www.fisherpaykel.com

Frigidaire (washer, dryer)
www.frigidaire.com

Seattle Tile Company (backsplashes)
https://seattletile.com

Minka-Aire (ceiling fan)
www.minkagroup.net

Kohler (sinks, toilets)
www.us.kohler.com

Hansgrohe (faucets, shower fixtures)
www.hansgrohe-usa.com

Pental Surfaces (countertops, flooring)
www.pentalonline.com

JamesHardie (fiber cement boards)
www.jameshardie.com

CONTEMPORARY FARMHOUSE
pp. 160–165

ARCHITECT/BUILDER

Unity Homes
https://unityhomes.com

PHOTOGRAPHER

James R. Salomon Photography
www.salomonphoto.com

SUPPLIERS

Mitsubishi Electric (mini-split air-source heat pump)
www.mitsubishicomfort.com

Navien (on-demand water heater)
www.navieninc.com

RenewAire (ERV)
www.renewaire.com

Kohler (plumbing fixtures)
www.us.kohler.com

Juno (lighting fixtures)
https://juno.acuitybrands.com

Kichler (lighting fixtures)
www.kichlerlightinglights.com

Sea Gull Lighting (lighting fixtures)
www.seagulllightingonline.com

Kenmore (appliances)
www.kenmore.com

Sherwin-Williams (paint)
www.sherwin-williams.com

Starmark (cabinets)
www.starmarkcabinetry.com

JamesHardie (fiber cement siding)
www.jameshardie.com

Intus Windows (triple-glazed tilt-turn windows)
www.intuswindows.com

Concrete Resurrection (concrete flooring)
https://concreteresurrection .com

Kährs (engineered wood)
www.kahrs.com/en-us

Emerson (outdoor ceiling fans)
www.emerson.com

CITY HOUSE ON THE RIVER
pp. 166–171

ARCHITECT

Anik Péloquin, Anik Péloquin Architecte
www.anikpeloquin.ca

BUILDER

Construction Fernand Martel
Saint-Eustache, Quebec, Canada

PHOTOGRAPHER

Alberto Biscaro
Quebec, Canada

SUPPLIERS

Benjamin Moore (paint)
www.benjaminmoore.com

Conserg Design + Fabrication (weathered-steel fence)
Marieville, Quebec, Canada

Sioux City Brick
https://siouxcitybrick.com

Les Industries I.S.A. (roasted outside wood)
www.portailconstructo.com/ batiguide/industries_isa_inc

Ébénisterie Claude Tourigny
(cabinetry)
Bécancour, Quebec, Canada

Abet Laminati (laminates)
https://abetlaminati.com/en

Granite R US (countertops)
www.graniterus.ca/en

JennAir (appliances)
https://v1.jennair.com

Broan (range hood)
https://broan.com

Céramique Royal (ceramic
tiles)
http://royalceramic.com

Marquis Collection (gas
fireplace)
https://marquisfireplaces.net

Unik Parquet (yellow birch
oiled wood flooring)
https://unikparquet.com/en

Plomberie F. Ravary (bathroom
fixtures)
www.plomberiefravary.ca/en

TOTO (toilet/bidet)
www.totousa.com

PASSIVE DACHA
pp. 172–177

ARCHITECT
GO Logic
www.gologic.us

PHOTOGRAPHER
Josh Gerritsen Media
http://joshgerritsen.com

SUPPLIERS
Canadian Solar (solar PV
panels)
www.canadiansolar.com

Kneer-Südfenster (triple-
glazed windows)
www.kneer-suedfenster.de/en

Zehnder (HRV)
https://zehnderamerica.com

Fischer & Paykel (dish drawer)
www.fisherpaykel.com

Asko (clothes washer)
www.askona.com

Nest (thermostat)
https://nest.com

Rinnai (tankless water heater)
www.rinnai.us

Simple Pump (hand pump)
www.simplepump.com/our-
pumps/hand-operated

MONTROSE PLACE
BUNGALOW
pp. 178–183

ARCHITECT
David Heide Design Studio
www.dhdstudio.com

BUILDER
Crown Construction Company
www.crownmn.com

PHOTOGRAPHER
Greg Page Photography
https://gregpagephotography
.com

SUPPLIERS
Wolf (stove)
www.subzero-wolf.com

Marvin (windows)
www.marvin.com

Rohl (kitchen sink)
https://rohlhome.com

Kohler (bathroom fixtures)
www.us.kohler.com

David Heide Design Studio
(lighting fixtures)
www.dhdstudio.com

Liebherr (refrigerator)
https://home.liebherr.com

JamesHardie (fiber cement
siding)
www.jameshardie.com

ENABLE BY
NORTHWESTERN
pp. 184–189

ARCHITECT/BUILDER
Students and faculty and
partners of Northwestern
University
www.northwestern.house

PHOTOGRAPHERS
Dennis Schroeder
Monika Wnuk
Josh Bauer
U.S. Department of Energy
Solar Decathlon

SUPPLIERS
Rockwool (mineral wool
insulation)
www.rockwool.com

GAF DecoTech (roof-integrated
solar panel system)
www.gaf.com/en-us/
residential-roofing/decotech

CertainTeed (AirRenew
drywall)
www.certainteed.com

Eco-Panels (polyurethane-
filled SIPs)
www.eco-panels.com

Beko (washer and dryer,
dishwasher, microwave,
refrigerator)
www.bekoappliances.com

Blomberg (electric oven and
cooktop)
www.blombergappliances.com

Niagara Conservation (toilet,
bathroom showerhead)
www.niagaraconservation.com

Chiltrix (air-source chiller heat
pump)
www.chiltrix.com

First Co. (variable-speed
hydronic air handler)
https://firstco.com

Schneider Electric (hybrid
inverter/charger, grid-tied
capacity, electric charging
station)
www.schneider-electric.us

SolarWorld (Sunmodule Plus
panels)
www.solarworld-usa.com

Sun Xtender (solar batteries)
www.sunxtender.com

American Standard (stainless-
steel kitchen sink)
www.americanstandard-us
.com

Kohler (kitchen faucets,
bathroom sink and faucets,
vanity)
www.us.kohler.com

Zehnder (ERV)
https://zehnderamerica.com

Pool & Spa Enclosures (Corso
Ultima moveable sunroom
enclosure)
www.sunrooms-enclosures
.com

Neptronic (programmable
thermostat)
www.neptronic.com

Nest (smoke alarm, learning
thermostat)
https://nest.com

Weyerhaeuser (PSL beams,
resistant to fungal decay and
termite attack)
www.weyerhaeuser.com

TruStile (doors)
www.trustile.com

DIRTT (Breathe Wall)
www.dirtt.net

PURETi (spray coating for
windows)
http://pureti.com

Awair (monitor for indoor air
quality)
https://getawair.com

Caséta by Lutron (lighting
fixture control)
www.casetawireless.com

Corning Willow Glass (kitchen
island stone print).
https://www.corning.com/
worldwide/en/innovation/
corning-emerging-innovations/
corning-willow-glass.html

Arbor Wood Co (thermally
modified timber)
http://arborwoodco.com

Crossville (tile in bathroom
walls/floor and entryway)
www.crossvilleinc.com

Solatube (skylight tubes)
www.solatube.com

Boral TruExterior Siding
(>70% recycled content,
including fly ash from coal
combustion)
www.boralamerica.com

THE JUST RIGHT HOUSE
pp. 190–195

ARCHITECT
Wolfworks
www.homesthatfit.com

PHOTOGRAPHER
Jamie Wolf/Wolfworks

PROJECT MANAGER
Janet Downey

SUPPLIERS
Schüco (windows, doors)
www.schueco.com/web2/us

Zehnder (HRV)
https://zehnderamerica.com

Mitsubishi Electric (mini-split
heat pump)
www.mitsubishicomfort.com

Bradford White (heat pump
water heater)
www.bradfordwhite.com

Aegis Solar Energy (PV
system)
www.aegis-solar.com

NAPA HOUSE
pp. 196–201

DESIGNER
LivingHomes
www.livinghomes.net

FABRICATOR
Plant Prefab, Inc.
www.plantprefab.com

CONTRACTOR
Bruce Tucker Construction
www.brucetuckerconstruction
.com

PHOTOGRAPHER
PlanOmatic
www.planomatic.com

SUPPLIERS
Marvin (Integrity windows and
doors)
www.marvin.com

Fujitsu (mini-split ductless
HVAC system)
www.fujitsu.com/us

Knauf Insulation (batt
insulation)
www.knaufinsulation.us

Daltile (recycled tiles)
www.daltile.com

Sunpower (solar panels)
https://us.sunpower.com

Kohler (sinks, faucets)
www.us.kohler.com

JamesHardie (siding)
www.jameshardie.com

Rheem (tankless water heater)
www.rheem.com

TOTO (toilet)
www.totousa.com

SunPak (stainless-steel
propane heaters)
www.alfresco-heating.com

Urbanfloor (Valentina oak
flooring)
www.urbanfloor.com

Star (propane four-burner
stove)
https://star-mfg.com

Hobart (commercial high-
temperature dishwasher)
www.hobartcorp.com

Mugnaini (wood-burning oven)
www.mugnaini.com

John Boos (deep, commercial-
size stainless-steel appliances)
https://johnboos.com

Central Restaurant Products
(refrigerator with counter
space for rolling out dough)
www.centralrestaurant.com

THE RACE RESIDENCE
pp. 202–209

ARCHITECT
Craig Race Architecture
https://craigrace.com

PHOTOGRAPHER
Robert Watson Photography
www.robertwatsonphotography
.com

SUPPLIERS
Benjamin Moore (low-VOC
paint)
www.benjaminmoore.com

Thermador (appliances)
www.thermador.com

Blanchon (floor varnish)
www.blanchon.co.uk

Internorm (windows)
www.internorm.com/en/
internorm

Mitsubishi Electric (air-source
heat pump)
www.mitsubishicomfort.com

Bio Flame (ethanol burner)
www.thebioflame.com

TOTEM HOUSE
pp. 210–215

ARCHITECT
Reza Aliabadi, Atelier RZLBD
http://rzlbd.com

CONSTRUCTION
MANAGEMENT
Urbanline Studio

PHOTOGRAPHER
Borzu Talaie
www.borxu.com

SUPPLIERS
Duravit (basin and toilet)
www.duravit.com

JennAir (cooktop)
https://v1.jennair.com

Frigidaire (appliances)
www.frigidaire.com

Sistemalux (lighting)
www.sistemalux.com

Nest (smart thermostat)
https://nest.com

GRANNY PAD
pp. 216–221

ARCHITECT
Best Practice Architecture
www.bestpracticearchitecture
.com

BUILDER
Kable Design Build
http://kabledesignbuild.com

PHOTOGRAPHER
Sozinho Imagery
www.sozinhoimagery.com

SUPPLIERS
IKEA (kitchen cabinets)
www.ikea.com

Daltile (tile)
www.daltile.com

Silestone (countertops)
www.silestoneusa.com

Blomberg (refrigerator, range,
washer, dryer)
www.blombergappliances.com

Benjamin Moore (paint)
www.benjaminmoore.com

Simpson Door Company
(Dutch door)
www.simpsondoor.com

Milgard Windows & Doors
(windows)
www.milgard.com

Velux (skylights)
www.veluxusa.com

ERICKSON HOUSE
pp. 222–227

ARCHITECT/MANUFACTURER
Stillwater Dwellings
http://stillwaterdwellings.com

CONTRACTOR
Dan Neumeyer, JADE
Craftsman Builders, LLC
www.jadecraftsmanbuilders
.com

PHOTOGRAPHER
Jeff Amram Photography
www.jeffamram.com

SUPPLIERS
Milgard Windows & Doors
(windows)
www.milgard.com

Sierra Pacific Windows
(windows, sliding glass doors)
www.sierrapacificwindows.com

WarmBoard (hydronic radiant
heating system)
www.warmboard.com

JamesHardie (fiber cement
siding)
www.jameshardie.com

Caesarstone (countertops)
www.caesarstoneus.com